MW00778801

The Modern Learning Ecosystem

A NEW L&D MINDSET FOR THE EVER-CHANGING WORKPLACE

JD Dillon

atd
PRESS

Alexandria, VA

© 2022 ASTD DBA the Association for Talent Development (ATD)

All rights reserved. Printed in the United States of America.

25 24 23 22   1 2 3 4 5

No part of this publication may be reproduced, distributed, or transmitted in any form or by any means, including photocopying, recording, information storage and retrieval systems, or other electronic or mechanical methods, without the prior written permission of the publisher, except in the case of brief quotations embodied in critical reviews and certain other noncommercial uses permitted by copyright law. For permission requests, please go to copyright.com, or contact Copyright Clearance Center (CCC), 222 Rosewood Drive, Danvers, MA 01923 (telephone: 978.750.8400; fax: 978.646.8600).

ATD Press is an internationally renowned source of insightful and practical information on talent development, training, and professional development.

ATD Press
1640 King Street
Alexandria, VA 22314 USA

Ordering information: Books published by ATD Press can be purchased by visiting ATD's website at td.org/books or by calling 800.628.2783 or 703.683.8100.

Library of Congress Control Number: 2022943361

ISBN-10: 1-953946-38-0
ISBN-13: 978-1-953946-38-6
e-ISBN: 978-1-953946-39-3

ATD Press Editorial Staff
Director: Sarah Halgas
Manager: Melissa Jones
Content Manager, Learning Sciences: Alexandria Clapp
Developmental Editor: Jack Harlow
Production Editor: Hannah Sternberg
Text Design: Shirley E.M. Raybuck
Cover Design: Rose Richey

Text Layout: Kathleen Dyson
Printed by BR Printers, California

To the frontline—for doing the heavy lifting
that keeps us all moving forward.
To Margaret, Joey, Nicole, and Carol—for giving me a shot.
To Stephanie—for always being there.
Thank you.

Contents

Preface

This book is a little different . . . because it's my story.

Before we get into it, I want to thank you for buying my book. Or, if you borrowed it from a peer, thanks for trusting them to make a super smart recommendation to aid your professional development. Or, if you won this book as a prize at a conference when you were really aiming for the latest version of the Apple Watch, my condolences. If it makes you feel any better, this book can also tell the time.

Unfortunately, it's only accurate twice a day.

See what I mean? This is going to be different.

There are so many great L&D books out there. I'm sure I'll reference *Make It Stick* by Peter Brown, Henry Roediger III, and Mark McDaniel several times before you hit the back cover. It's the first book every L&D professional should read. Then there's *Design for How People Learn* by Julie Dirksen, the most dog-eared book in the biz. Reuben Tozman's *Learning On Demand* totally changed the way I think about learning in the workplace.

I want this reading experience to stand out. I want it to feel like we're having a conversation, so I wrote just like I talk in real life. I also hope this book lives beyond your first (hopefully complete) read as an ongoing reference guide. My goal is to help you and your peers think differently about the role of learning in the workplace and how you apply proven practices to help people do their jobs better every day. But mostly, I want to geek out with you about cool L&D ideas. I hope that's OK with you!

This is my first real book. By that, I mean it's the first time I've ever written this many words in one place. I've published hundreds of magazine articles, online columns, and blog posts. I've dropped dozens of podcasts, livestreams, and videos. I've delivered somewhere around 1,000 presentations during my 20+ years in corporate learning and operations. I'm always grateful to have the opportunity to share my ideas and perspective with professional peers like you.

If you've heard me speak or read something I've written before, you may have seen me explore a variety of L&D topics: Microlearning. Adaptive learning. Artificial intelligence. Gamification. Data. Curation. Technology ecosystems. I touch upon several of these topics in this book too. But no matter the topic, my content always has one thing in common: stories. Stories make me more than just a guy with an idea and a publisher. They make me part of the L&D community. They show that I've done the work, that I've failed more than I've succeeded, and that I've learned along the way. This book includes lots of personal stories and reflections.

Several chapters open with a story about a time I faced a particularly daunting learning and performance challenge. I explain the steps I took to overcome these disruptions and what I figured out about modern workplace learning practices along the way. I've managed to duct-tape together an L&D methodology through years of experimentation and doing the best with what I had available. This book explains how I did that.

There's one more thing I want to mention before we dive into the good stuff. You don't have to read the entire book front to back to get value from it. If you're new to the profession or trying to figure out how to reshape your organization's approach to learning and performance, I suggest starting at the beginning and consuming the story in sequence. The concepts build upon one another—moving from philosophy to framework to application. On the other hand, if you're an experienced professional trying to overcome a specific disruption or fix a specific problem within your learning ecosystem, jump to the chapters that are most relevant to you. The main concepts stand on their own and each chapter offers plenty of practical suggestions to enhance your problem-solving efforts. I also added Spoiler Alerts at the start of each chapter so you'll know what's going to be covered.

So thanks again for buying/borrowing/winning my first book! I hope it helps you provide even more value to your organization and the people you support. And I hope you chuckle a few times along the way, even if it's sometimes at my expense.

Now, let's commence with the AHAs and HAHAs with my first story.

Introduction

Please Stand Clear of the Doors: How Disruption Changed My Perspective on Learning

I spent the first eight years of my career as an operations manager in movie theaters and theme parks. When you were out having fun with your friends and family, my frontline teams and I were serving you popcorn and loading you onto your favorite rides.

My first L&D role was as a project consultant and classroom facilitator at the Walt Disney World Resort. I had always loved Disney growing up, and all my childhood vacations took place in Orlando, Florida. It made total sense that, when it was time to leave Philadelphia for college and explore a bit more of the world, I chose the school closest to Disney. I attended the University of Central Florida, graduating with a degree in communications and marketing. A few years later, I picked up a second job working part-time on my weekends at Disney. My 10-year career with the company began at Star Tours, where I shuttled guests off to the Forest Moon of Endor.

I worked side by side with the Muppets and Indiana Jones. I dressed up like a cowboy and screamed things like "yeehaw" and "saddle up and ride" in front of complete strangers at the Great Movie Ride—my favorite attraction as a kid. I rapidly cross-trained my way into management roles in custodial and operations before landing my first L&D gig as part of the largest training initiative in company history. For three years, I ran around a campus the size of San Francisco designing and delivering instructor-led courses and interactive experiences focused on guest service. It was the most fun I've ever had (and will probably *ever* have) at work.

Then I got my first real taste of workplace disruption thanks to developments captured in the book and film titled *The Big Short*. In 2009, support functions were cut as a result of an economic recession. I was lucky enough to keep my job, but I was sent back into operations where I managed the two busiest and most popular attractions in the world's busiest theme park (Big Thunder Mountain Railroad and Splash Mountain in the Magic Kingdom Park). I hung around for a few more years, eventually exiting after spending time as a seasonal skipper at the world-famous Jungle Cruise. It was a tough decision, but it was the right thing to do for my career.

I got a new role supporting instructional design and technology for a US-based network of contact centers. It wasn't exactly the most magical place on Earth, but it was a chance to fully pursue an L&D career. While I had a few years of L&D experience, I still hadn't done much beyond instructor-led and on-the-job training. This was my opportunity to try my hand at digital learning within a large, distributed organization. I moved across town. I got engaged. Everything in my life changed over the course of six months.

Knock knock!
Who's there?
Unexpected workplace disruption.
Unexpected workplace disruption who?

I was just getting the hang of contact center operations when the company decided to "right size." Half of the people working in my building were laid off that day. Thankfully, I made it through again, but the restructure dramatically changed my responsibilities. I was hired to support one department with 2,000 employees. Now I had to figure out how to support 10,000 people across the entire country. More responsibility, fewer resources. Sound familiar?

Disruption is a recurring theme in my L&D career and throughout this book. You can see some disruptions coming from a mile away—like the impact streaming entertainment is having on movie theaters and cable companies. Other disruptions are sudden and unexpected—like when you have to move your entire company to working remotely because a global pandemic shut down day-to-day life. Did I mention I started writing this book six weeks after the COVID-19 pandemic first put the US into lockdown?

In every case, disruption forces us to think differently about how we do the things we do, whether that's designing learning programs or shopping for groceries. This book is a summary of everything I've learned while continuously reimagining the way I do my work over the past 15 years. From my first big workplace disruption at Disney to my current work with frontline employers around the world as Axonify's chief learning architect, I've been forced to reflect on my perspective time and time again. Does the way I do things make sense? Do my principles and tactics apply in this world? Am I still relevant to the people I'm trying to help?

Nothing in my career compares to this latest disruption, and I had a hard time answering these questions in the middle of 2020. That's part of the reason it took me so long to write this book. I didn't want to assume it was worthwhile in a world of work that was in the middle of this much change. So I reached out to the global L&D community. I spoke with retailers in New Zealand, grocers in Canada, and financial services teams in South Africa. We talked about how their organizations were managing to keep pace and work their way through this kind of disruption.

Some were faring better than others, and I noticed that the ones who were succeeding all had something in common. It wasn't a specific training program or technology. Each of these companies had faced significant disruption in the few years leading up to the pandemic. They had expanded their perspectives, gone beyond traditional courses, and adopted an ecosystem mindset as the core of their learning strategies. Now these systems and practices were standing up against the biggest wave of economic, social, and political change in modern history. They didn't mean to do it, but they were applying the same tactics I had adopted 12 years earlier to battle my own workplace disruption.

That's who this book is for—L&D teams who are struggling to keep pace with change, who recognize the shortcomings of traditional training tactics, and who know they need to change but just don't know where to start.

This book will help shift your learning mindset and create a learning and performance ecosystem that's ready for anything.

First, we'll establish the purpose of L&D in the modern workplace and explore existing themes and concepts that are critical for adopting a modern learning mindset (chapters 1–2).

Next, we'll break down the Modern Learning Ecosystem (MLE) Framework. This framework presents a new way to align your L&D tactics so you can help employees solve today's biggest problems while building the knowledge and skills they'll need to be successful in the future (chapters 3–10).

Last, we'll cover considerations like measurement, technology, and influence that will prove critical in your ability to shift your organization's perspective on and approach to workplace learning (chapters 11–14).

Are you ready to get started? Feeling good? Need a restroom break? No? Alright, let's go!

Chapter 1

Time for a Remix

Take Inspiration From the Models That Came Before

We're going to explore three workplace learning and performance models that heavily influenced my L&D practices and inspired my own framework. It's time for a quick refresh on:

- The 70-20-10 Model
- The Continuous Learning Model
- The 5 Moments of Need

> *"There is no such thing as a new idea. It is impossible. We simply take a lot of old ideas and put them into a sort of mental kaleidoscope. We give them a turn and they make new and curious combinations. We keep on turning and making new combinations indefinitely; but they are the same old pieces of colored glass that have been in use through all the ages."*
> —Mark Twain, *Mark Twain's Own Autobiography: The Chapters From the North American Review* (2010)

At least one chapter in every business book must begin with a quote from a highly regarded intellectual. I figured I'd get mine out of the way early!

Of course, ole Sam Clemens is absolutely right. You rarely run into a genuinely new idea. Take movies for example. Nowadays, everything seems like a reboot (who's playing Batman right now?) or a remake (but I've already seen *The Lion King*!). Even movies that aren't officially reboots or remakes rehash the same themes and story tropes over and over again. This is why my 10th grade class spent an entire month studying *Hamlet*. You can apply its themes to answer all possible literature questions on advanced placement (AP) tests because every story has already been done.

The same is true for the learning profession. The fundamentals of how people learn have not changed in a long, long time. What has evolved is the context in which people are required to learn and apply their skills. We weren't built to handle the pace of change work throws at us, so we have to find new ways to connect the old dots and overcome this challenge. This is what we're going to do for most of this book. We're not going to reboot or remake L&D. Instead, we're going to rethink how we apply proven practices to solve familiar problems. I'm going to share the best of what I've learned over the last 20 years to help you connect old dots in new ways. Together, we're going to remix L&D.

I'd love to tell you that everything in this book is the result of me being really strategic and forward-thinking; that this all came about when I went into my office one day, closed the door, thought really hard, covered a dry erase board in ideas, and emerged with a fully formed methodology. That's not what happened. I've always figured things out through experimentation, sharing, and conversation. My career is based on trying lots of stuff, keeping what works, and trying it again. I continue to pick up new ideas along the way and give them a spin to see how they mesh with my existing practices. Only in retrospect have I realized that I developed my own framework for addressing workplace learning and performance challenges. More on that later!

I've read a lot of articles, listened to a lot of podcasts, and attended a lot of education sessions. An untold number of people who are much smarter than me have influenced my work. For example, Reuben Tozman's *Learning On Demand* was the first L&D book I ever read. It completely reshaped the way I thought about my job.

I expect you'll have several "this sounds a lot like . . ." moments as you read this book. You may even identify sources of inspiration that I've never come across in my own work. That said, three particular concepts are clearly reflected in my approach to workplace learning. I didn't build

my framework to specifically align with these concepts. H/
ing back, each model inspired the way I look at the role of

The 70-20-10 Model

70-20-10 Towards 100% Performance by Jos Arets, Charles Jennings, and
Vivian Heijnen is the best coffee table book in our profession. The content is great. The design is awesome. And, much like Kramer's coffee
table book about coffee tables in Seinfeld, the hardback publication is
also sturdy enough to act as furniture.

Besides ADDIE (analyze, design, development, implement, evaluate)
and the Kirkpatrick Model (four layers of measurement), I hear people
reference 70-20-10 more than any other L&D concept. You probably
already know it well. But, just in case you need it, here's a quick summary (Figure 1-1):

- 70 percent of what we learn comes from **experience**.
- 20 percent of what we learn comes from **interacting with others**.
- 10 percent of what we learn comes from **formal learning
  programs**.

Figure 1-1. The 70-20-10 Model

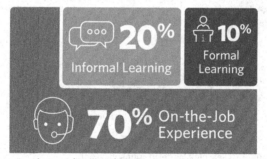

Adapted from Arets, Jennings, and Heijnen (2016).

People learn by doing a lot more than just courses, which make up
a very small part of the workplace learning experience. That's the gist of
it, but you should still read *70-20-10 Towards 100% Performance*. Over the
years, I've heard plenty of people argue about the numbers, which were
not meant to be scientifically accurate. I've also watched people attempt

ply the model way too literally. For example, a peer once designed a aining program using these exact ratios for certain kinds of activities, which is beside the point. The numbers are given more as estimates, and are meant to represent how people learn, not how programs should be designed. That's why we need another model to refine these ideas a little bit—and that's up next.

The Continuous Learning Model

Before I wrote this book, I honestly thought this one was called the 4 Es. Apparently, its real name is the Continuous Learning Model (Figure 1-2). This is probably the concept I see referenced the most without citation in the profession. You've probably seen the visual with the four concentric circles, but did you know the model first appeared in a research bulletin written in December 2014 by Dani Johnson, former research manager for Bersin by Deloitte and current co-founder of RedThread Research?

Figure 1-2. Continuous Learning Model

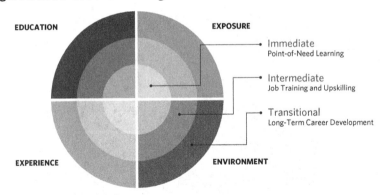

Adapted from Continuous Learning Model in Johnson (2014).

The Continuous Learning Model was created in response to L&D's imprecise application of 70-20-10. It didn't seek to contradict 70-20-10. Instead, it tried to further expand workplace learning beyond the boundaries of programmatic training. The model focuses on "structuring resources, expectations, and learning culture in such a way as to encourage employees to learn continuously throughout their tenure with the organization." The Es include:

- **Education:** The structured activities that often comprise the bulk of workplace learning strategy
- **Experience:** Practical, hands-on activities that occur within the workflow
- **Exposure:** Learning that occurs during interactions with peers, experts, and coaches
- **Environment:** Tools and systems that make up the infrastructure that enables organizational learning

We haven't even started talking about my framework, and we're already remixing some of the most popular concepts in the industry. Why stop now? Let's add one more.

The 5 Moments of Need

File this one under "It's so obvious that it's brilliant." Bob Mosher and Conrad Gottfredson built an entire practice around the 5 Moments of Need and their approach to performance support (Figure 1-3). The moments include:

- Learning to do something new for the first time
- Expanding the depth of one's existing knowledge
- Recalling how to correctly apply knowledge in the moment of need
- Using knowledge to solve a timely problem
- Adapting one's existing knowledge in the face of change

Figure 1-3. The 5 Moments of Need

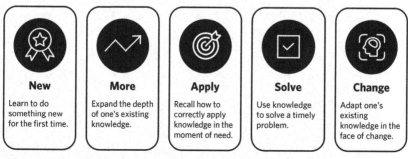

Adapted from Gottfredson and Mosher (2021).

Think about when you need help figuring something out at work. It probably aligns with one of those five moments, each of which carries its own set of considerations when designing right-fit support solutions.

Finding the Red Thread

Have you figured out what 70-20-10, the Continuous Learning Model, and the 5 Moments of Need have in common? Reality. They don't overcomplicate the concept of learning. They don't get deep in the weeds on how to design specific solutions. Instead, they reflect the fundamental realities of how learning works. They may seem like common sense, but they highlight what is often missing in organizational learning and development.

When it comes to remixes, Mark Twain said, "We simply take a lot of old ideas and put them into a sort of mental kaleidoscope." Models and frameworks provide a lens through which we can reshape our view of how we live and work. Some models, such as ADDIE, shift our view toward the programmatic side of learning. Others, like the 5 Moments of Need, shift our view towards the everyday workflow. The Modern Learning Ecosystem framework presented in this book will provide another lens. It will help you see the role of organizational learning from a new angle—one that's just as realistic, practical, and continuous as the models that inspired it. Plus, it's grounded in the most consequential issue facing today's workforce: disruption.

Chapter 2

Down the Rabbit Hole

Shift Your Mindset Before Shifting Your Strategy

SPOILER ALERT

We're going to explore powerful themes influencing the way organizations think about workplace learning, including the push to modernize L&D and the growing importance of skills within enterprise talent strategies. It's time to answer questions like:

- What is the real purpose of L&D?
- What does it mean to adopt a modern learning mindset?
- What will it take to close the skills gap?

Are you ready for whatever comes next?

That probably sounds like an unfair question. No one really knows what's coming next. Even the most well-informed plans get sidetracked by unexpected events. One day, you're focused on a big product release. The next, you're dealing with a sudden regulatory change. It's L&D's job to help people always be ready for whatever's coming down the pike. That's what makes this profession so exciting . . . and so frustrating!

Disruption has long been a major influence on L&D because it's a never-ending workplace reality. It is inescapable in every industry, and it's only accelerating. According to Accenture's 2019 *Breaking Through Disruption* report, 71 percent of the 10,000 companies analyzed were either in the middle or on the brink of significant disruption. And that's before disruption fundamentally changed people's relationships with work in 2020. Companies are just now getting a clear picture of their current challenges. Only 6 percent are highly confident in their ability to foresee and respond to future disruption, according to Accenture's *Business Futures 2021 Report*.

Some industries are often thought of as more susceptible to disruption than others. Consider the way e-commerce has shaken the foundations of the retail business since the mid-2000s. Fleeting stability is now a common feeling in many organizations, regardless of their industry, scale, or market penetration. Just ask Blockbuster, Pets.com, Kodak, and MySpace, all of whom were, at one point or another, dominant players in their spaces. There is no such thing as a disruption-proof company.

Disruption affects everyone within an organization, but it can feel different depending on where you sit. For executives, it feels like stock price volatility and extra pressure from the board of directors. For management, it feels like cost reductions, priority adjustments, and a constant demand to get more done with fewer resources. On the frontline, it feels like employment uncertainty, overwhelming workloads, and unanswered questions. I've always found myself stuck right in the middle as an L&D pro. We're expected to help stakeholders execute their changing mandates while also supporting employees by providing the why and how. Rarely do we have all the answers. However, there's one thing we know for sure:

> An organization can only transform as fast as its people
> can learn.

The Coyote Conundrum

Do you feel like you're always chasing the next thing as an L&D pro?

It's our job to make sure other people can effectively do theirs, but knowledge and skill expectations are moving targets. I've always compared L&D to a certain cartoon coyote who's spent his entire on-screen existence trying to catch a certain cartoon bird (their names have been redacted because I want Warner Bros. to let me watch the next Batman movie). The coyote has a plan. He has the best ACME-brand tools. But the same thing always happens at the end of every episode. The coyote falls off a cliff and gets nailed in the head with an anvil. Talk about adding insult to injury!

Has your job ever made you feel just like the coyote? You had a great plan. It was blessed by every stakeholder and executive. You were ready to implement it when all the sudden . . . the world changed. Your Very Important Project was suddenly no longer very important. And then you're right back at the beginning of the episode, chasing the organization's next big priority.

This is just the way business works today. Change is inevitable. We can't stop it. Our only choice is to embrace and adapt to it. We must think differently about how we do our jobs within the context of a perpetually changing workplace. We must step back and rethink the role L&D should play in enabling organizational transformation. Luckily, we can look to the coyote for another important lesson!

Why has the coyote been so unsuccessful for so long? His problem is simple: He's hungry. On paper, it makes sense to go after the obvious solution: the bird right in front of him. But that's his real mistake! He never should have started chasing the bird at all. He was never going to catch it, no matter how many tools he threw at the problem. Instead, he should have paused, taken a step back, and reassessed both the problem and his own capabilities. He should have found a new way to solve the problem. He should have become a professional painter.

What?!

The coyote is pretty bad at everything he does. However, he does possess one stand-out skill. Remember how he would often paint the opening of a fake tunnel on a rock in an attempt to trick the bird into slamming head-first into it, rendering it unconscious and easier to catch? Unfortunately, the fake tunnel always turned into a real tunnel, allowing the bird to speed right through and evade capture. That's it! That's what the coyote missed! The dude had the skill to paint fake tunnels that turn into real tunnels! He should have applied this skill to secure a few sweet government infrastructure contracts, rapidly increasing his personal wealth and making sure he never had to chase down his dinner ever again.

This must be the most ridiculous section of any L&D book ever written. But there is a valuable point to be learned from my cartoonish observation. L&D cannot keep up with the pace of change if we keep applying the same old strategies. Instead, we must step back and reevaluate our methods. We must ask hard questions, challenge our assumptions, and find new ways to apply our skills. What do we really do? And how does this relate to what people really need to perform at their best in today's workplace?

A Crisis of Purpose

What do you call your L&D department?

I've been witness to some spectacular wordsmithing over the years. My first L&D role was in "Operations Training." Simple. Straightforward. Then, we changed our name to "Operations, Learning, and Development" because we did more than just training. Later on, I was part of "Support Training and Multimedia Projects" or STAMP for short. I've been a chief learning architect, principle learning strategist, learning experience designer, and talent development director. I've made up most of my own titles, and yet I still can't explain what I do for a living to people outside this profession.

There's a reason you've never met an accountant who refers to themself as an "evidentiary actuarial inquisitor." Their profession has a clear purpose. Everyone understands the role they play within an organization, and they play that role consistently. People outside finance may not understand exactly what they do, but they acknowledge their purpose and respect their value. Accountants don't need to over-inflate their job titles or department names to get their point across. How would your stakeholders answer the question, "What does L&D do?" Would their answer match your own? Would it highlight the full value you believe your team brings to the organization?

L&D is a unique profession. Everyone has an opinion on how we do what we do. People went to school and completed job training, so they believe they know what works. Accountants are left alone to account, but L&D pros are told to provide a 90-minute instructor-led course based on a 300-slide PowerPoint presentation next Thursday. It's not fair, but it's our reality. An easy way to compensate is to change our team names and job titles. We use terms like *learning experience architect* to remind people that we're experts in this stuff. Unfortunately, credibility has little to do with names. Right now, the four most valuable public companies in the world are named after a fruit (Apple), a portmanteau (Microsoft), a rainforest (Amazon), and letters (Alphabet). Identity is derived from value, not vice-versa. We must shift our mindsets if we want to become vital, respected contributors.

The Modern Learning Mindset

I spent a lot of time in 2020 and 2021 speaking with HR and L&D professionals around the world. I wanted to understand how they were helping people get through the changes caused by the pandemic. I met with managers, influencers, analysts, and practitioners in retail, hospitality, healthcare, technology, manufacturing, pharmaceuticals, grocery, telecommunications, and professional services. Unsurprisingly, I found that no one was prepared for this level of disruption.

However, I noticed that some organizations were handling the situation a little better than others. They seemed to respond to changes more quickly and kept their businesses moving forward and their employees safe and productive. They had rapidly adopted new practices, such as remote work, e-commerce, and home delivery. They worked in different industries. They applied different tools and strategies. But they all had one thing in common: mindset. Every standout organization was in the process of adopting what I call a *modern learning mindset* prior to the onset of the pandemic. They didn't know it at the time, but they were setting themselves up to face the ultimate workplace disruption.

What exactly is a modern learning mindset? Well, *modern* is an odd term because it's a perpetually moving target. What's modern today will be antiquated tomorrow. This is why the term so accurately describes the mindset L&D pros must adopt in today's workplace. Our strategies must be grounded by the desire to overcome the sudden and violent impact of change. Our tools and tactics will evolve over time, but the fundamental principles that inform "the way we do things" must be durable and disruption-ready. These principles must inform our most important decisions, including technology purchases, solution design, and skill development. Every L&D team must apply the six principles that have helped exemplary organizations "sur-thrive" during a time of unprecedented change.

Principle 1. Make Learning an Essential Part of the Work(flow)

Time is the biggest obstacle to learning—full stop. LinkedIn Learning reiterated this point when they found that executives and managers agree that getting employees to make time for learning is the number one challenge for talent development (LinkedIn 2018). This is especially true in frontline workspaces, such as contact centers, manufacturing facilities, and retail stores, where employees are heavily scheduled and cannot make time for focused development. Regardless of industry or role, people already have too much to do and not enough time to do it. How can they possibly fit classroom sessions and online courses into their schedules?

L&D teams that acknowledge this reality adopt strategies that fit within the flow of work. Microlearning has become a popular tactic because it helps L&D deliver short, focused training activities that are easier to consume during a busy workday. Of course, making content shorter doesn't mean people will automatically want to consume it. L&D must go beyond the idea of "learning in the flow of work" and build the business case for making learning part of the work itself. A modern learning mindset requires that organizations hold people accountable for learning just as they do for performance. They prioritize knowledge and skill development and continuously make the necessary investments to ensure people have time to dedicate to learning. They also recognize people for their efforts to develop themselves as well as supporting the development of others.

Principle 2. Take Advantage of the Full Ecosystem

How often do the people you support access your LMS? Once per month? Once per quarter? Only when they're chased down to complete compliance training? L&D's potential impact is artificially limited by our reliance on our own tools. Most people don't have to use a learning platform to do their jobs. This is why it takes so much poking and prodding to increase engagement . . . and way too much clicking for the user after they do log in.

People use a wide variety of tools to do their jobs. Retail associates use points of sale (POS) and handheld scanners. Professional salespeople use iPads and customer relationship management (CRM) systems. Delivery drivers use smartphones and navigation devices. A modern learning mindset pushes L&D to leverage the full range of tools, tactics, and systems available within the workflow to help people improve their performance. Why ask a deli worker to leave their position and walk to the back of the grocery store to access online content via a desktop computer in the office if the tablet they use in the department is fully capable of hosting the same training?

Principle 3. Apply Data to Accelerate Decision Making

Stakeholders have dictated my L&D priorities for most of my career. Even when I was able to decide which solutions to build, I was still playing the role of order-taker. To level the playing field and become a true business partner, I had to get ahead of the change and find ways to proactively identify knowledge and skills gaps within my audience. I had to get better with data so I could generate my own insights and address performance issues before they negatively affected my organizations. Improving data practices also helps L&D continuously assess the effectiveness of our solutions and adjust our strategies to maximize results.

L&D cannot move forward until we fix our measurement problem. Traditional models and approaches just don't work. If they did, we'd have stopped talking about this topic 30 years ago. Satisfaction surveys and test scores cannot help you identify and prioritize your organization's learning needs. This is why 69 percent of companies say that the inability to measure learning impact represents a challenge to achieving critical learning outcomes (Brandon Hall Group 2019). To adopt a modern learning mindset, L&D must prioritize measurement and solidify its data collection, analysis, and application practices.

Principle 4. Provide a Personal Experience at Scale

The audience-to-L&D ratio rarely works in our favor. Even well-resourced teams with more than 300 L&D pros usually support distributed audiences made up of 200,000 or more people across multiple brands and lines of business. Our ability to provide each person with the right support is overwhelmed by the size, scale, and complexity of our organizations. As a result, we apply generalized solutions and off-the-shelf courses that are intended to be one-size-fits-all but are in reality wrong-size-fits-none.

A modern learning mindset is grounded in the belief that everyone—regardless of role, background, status, tenure, or location—needs *and* deserves right-fit support so they can do their best work every day. To get there, L&D must rethink our strategies and overcome the challenge of scale to provide personalized solutions that meet each individual where they are in their development. This is a difficult problem to solve, but it's definitely possible thanks to modern data and technology practices.

Principle 5. Drive Clear Business Impact

If you cannot determine the impact of a learning solution, there is no point in delivering it. *Impact* can mean a lot of different things in the workplace. Increasing sales revenue is an impact. Decreasing injury rates is an impact. Maintaining regulatory compliance is an impact. Increasing employee satisfaction is an impact. Learning, however, is not an impact. It's a potential means to achieve one.

People don't go to work to *learn*. They go to work to *do*. A modern learning mindset requires L&D to align our strategies with this reality and focus on how we affect performance outcomes. If we can't identify a measurable result—specifically how a solution will help people do their jobs better or enable the organization to achieve its goals—then we shouldn't waste our resources on the topic because we'll never be able to determine if it was worth it.

Principle 6. Foster Persistent Organizational Agility

How long does it take your L&D team to deploy a solution? The answer likely varies based on the intended audience and solution format. It takes a lot less time to develop a job aid for one department compared to building a full-fledged training program for an entire organization. That's the point. L&D must have the mechanisms in place to rapidly deploy right-size solutions at the speed stakeholders require. If the company announced a major process change today, could you get the necessary information in the hands of your employees by tomorrow?

Every organization has a learning culture. It's not something you build. It's something you foster. The problem is that many organizations have paid very little attention to their learning cultures. A modern learning mindset is L&D's key to reinvigorating this culture. It reestablishes the connection between learning and agility. It helps the organization transform more quickly and effectively because people are enabled to do the same.

Where Do You Stand?

Do you have a modern learning mindset? What about your L&D peers? Your stakeholders? The people you support? Do they consider learning a critical workplace strategy, or is it just a box that has to be checked so they can move along to more important things? We'll explore tactics you can apply to influence people throughout your organization to think differently about the role of learning in the workplace in later chapters. For now, use the questionnaire in Table 2-1 to conduct an honest assessment of your team's learning mindset.

Conduct this assessment with your L&D peers as well as a selection of your stakeholders. This will show how well aligned your organization is (or is not) with regards to the purpose and value of learning. Every organization is in a different place when it comes to building a modern learning ecosystem, but the first step is always the same. To start the shift from order-taker to performance partner, L&D must be willing to acknowledge that we've been focused on the wrong things for far too long.

Table 2-1. Where Do You Stand?

	Never	Sometimes	Always	Don't Know
Do we make sure people can find time within the flow of work for focused learning and development activity?				
Do we leverage a meaningful range of tools and tactics to help people access learning and support resources within their everyday workflows?				
Are we able to access and apply the data needed to proactively identify, prioritize, and address workplace learning and performance challenges?				
Do we meet people where they are in their individual development and help them efficiently close their personal knowledge and skills gaps?				
Do we identify the intended business impact of our learning solutions and measure their effectiveness based on our ability to achieve these expected results?				
Do we provide learning solutions that play a critical role in enabling organizational transformation at the speed and scale required?				

The Reskilling Paradox

I've been keeping a secret from you until this point: This book isn't actually about learning. It's about helping people keep up with change. You've certainly heard the phrase "the only thing constant in life is change" used to rally people around a big strategic shift. It may be an overused platitude, but it's also true. Thanks, Heraclitus!

L&D's mission must shift from a focus on learning to providing the support needed to help people do and be their best—today and tomorrow. This means we must become experts in our ability to help people navigate their way through change. We are a critical nexus in the workplace. We act as a conduit between those who know (management, subject matter experts, regulators) and those who need (employees, partners, students). Often, changes are routine and predictable, such as a new product release or annual compliance certification. But sometimes, they're sudden and unwieldy, such as a global health crisis. Regardless of the size or speed of change, one thing is always true: It's our job to prepare others so they can do their best work despite the change.

As we've already established, an organization can only transform as fast as its people can learn. Companies leave themselves open to added risk when they fail to prioritize and invest in learning and development. If the business is expected to evolve continuously to remain competitive, then the people within the business must always be learning. However, this is often the opposite of how organizations operate, especially during times of significant change. I've witnessed this firsthand over and over again. As times get tough, priorities shift, and budgets tighten, L&D and HR programs get cut. Managers push back by telling you that people don't have time for learning. Sure, this mindset may provide short-term boosts in operational capacity. But it has also contributed to one of the biggest problems in the global workplace: the skills gap.

Here's a set of obligatory stats related to the skills gap that you've probably seen before:

- 65 percent of organizations reported significant gaps in critical skill areas in 2020 according to the Fosway Group's report *The Reskilling Revolution.*
- 94 percent of business leaders expect employees to pick up new skills on the job according to *The Future of Jobs Report 2020* from the World Economic Forum.
- 17 percent of executives say their workers are very ready to adapt, reskill, and assume new roles according to Deloitte's 2021 *Human Capital Trends Report.*
- 46 percent of employees say their organizations reduced upskilling and reskilling opportunities during the pandemic according to Degreed's *The State of Skills 2021.*
- 41 percent of frontline employees say their companies offer any kind of future-focused skill development training.

How do these observations relate to the shortcomings in learning investment?

1. Organizations need people with new and in-demand skills to remain competitive.
2. Management knows they don't have enough of those people.
3. Management cuts back on skill development opportunities during times of change.

Good luck figuring this one out, L&D!

Closing the Right Gap

Imagine you came home to find your basement flooding. What is the first thing you would do?

a) Grab a bucket and start bailing.

b) Shut off the broken pipe.

c) Call a plumber.

B is the obviously correct answer. It's basic cause and effect. To overcome the effect (soggy belongings), you must identify and address the cause (busted plumbing). If you get distracted by the outcome and ignore the cause, you'll end up with an involuntary indoor swimming pool. This same problem is happening in the workplace when it comes to the skills conversation.

Managers have always expected people to possess the skills needed to do their jobs correctly. However, these skill requirements are constantly changing as organizations evolve. Some skills, such as core human behaviors like decision-making and collaboration, are more durable while others, such as those related to specific processes and technologies, are more perishable. This is why L&D exists and why we build volumes of content to help people learn how to do their jobs. So, if everyone already knows that skills are very important in the workplace, why are we suddenly talking about a massive skills gap?

We're looking at this issue from the wrong perspective. In fact, *there is no skills gap*. Yes, I know what the World Economic Forum said, and they are absolutely correct. Organizations don't have enough people with the right skills. But here's the thing: They never did. Unless you're the organization that's causing the disruption and creating the demand for a particular skill, you're always chasing. However, until recently, a combination of formal education, traditional job training, and practical experience was enough to develop the required skills. Now, the pace of change is just too fast. Universities aren't teaching the skills businesses need because they weren't important or didn't even exist a few years ago. People are expected to perform right out of the gate and therefore don't have time to figure things out on their own. Workplace training can take weeks or months to implement and then adds even more disruption to an already-overwhelmed operation.

The perceived skills gap is the effect. Water has been rushing into our basements for years, and the level is just now starting to rise over our heads. In this metaphor, the cause (broken pipe) is the *opportunity gap* (Figure 2-1). Organizations have failed to recognize the critical nature of learning as a key driver of business strategy for too long. Now, we're all dealing with the repercussions.

Figure 2-1. The Opportunity Gap

Opportunity gap may be a new term for you, but it's actually an amalgamation of several all-too-familiar challenges:

- **The mindset gap** represents how the organization, including everyone from frontline employees to senior management, views the role of learning within the workplace (which we discussed earlier). Is learning seen as a critical business capability or just a series of boxes people are required to check?

- **The priority gap** reflects how the organization does or does not prioritize learning as part of the everyday workflow. Are people permitted the time, capacity, and autonomy to focus on their development, or does this always get sidelined by the next business priority?
- **The inclusion gap** refers to how effectively everyone—regardless of role, tenure, background, demographic, status, education, or location—is included in an organization's learning strategy. Does every person have consistent access to meaningful growth opportunities, or is development limited to select groups?
- **The reality gap** explores how well L&D understands the day-to-day context of the people we support and our willingness to shift learning strategy accordingly. Do you build training that can be experienced during the limited time available in a busy workday, or do people have to adjust how they do their jobs to fit training in?
- **The digital gap** measures how consistently and effectively the organization invests in the technology needed to scale meaningful learning and support opportunities to the entire workforce. Can people access the resources they need to do their best work using the tools available within the workflow, including their personal devices if applicable?

Just like skills, these challenges are far from new. However, they are usually discussed in isolation, without consideration for the way they collectively create gaps in the employee experience, limit skill development, and reduce organizational agility.

The bad news is that we're still talking about systemic issues that have plagued workplace learning for decades. The good news: Adopting a modern mindset is the first step to finally bridging the opportunity gap. Now, it's time to introduce the framework that will help you take the next step toward architecting a disruption-ready learning ecosystem.

Chapter 3
The Proof Is in the Plumbing
Help Learning Flow Freely With the MLE Framework

SPOILER ALERT

We're going to introduce the framework on which this entire book is based (and make some sick analogies along the way). Yeah, this is a pretty awesome chapter! Get ready for:

- The six things L&D really does
- The Modern Learning Ecosystem Framework explained
- Why it's time to shift from programmatic L&D to systematic L&D

Yes, we're sticking with the stellar plumbing metaphor! But this time, the water isn't a stand-in for a business disruption that's flooding our fictitious organizational basements. Instead, water is a stand-in for learning.

Water is super useful. It resolves thirst. It washes hands. It extinguishes Class A fires. And thanks to modern plumbing, people can often access water when and where they need it to solve specific problems. If you need to water your lawn, you can attach a hose or sprinkler to the faucet outside your house and turn it on. If you need to do a load of laundry, water flows directly into the washing machine. We've created systems that make water access convenient, timely, and reliable for people who are lucky to have it.

Now consider a house without modern plumbing. The same problems still exist: dried out grass, dirty laundry, and so on. But now you have to haul the water from the source to the points of need. This means you're more likely to weigh the effort against the value. If the kitchen is on fire, you'll likely make the effort to move the water because it's a major problem. However, many other issues may not get resolved nearly as quickly . . . or at all. You may rely on rain to water the lawn and not worry about the appearance of the grass. Water remains just as useful without plumbing, but it's a lot harder to integrate it into everyday life without this modern convenience.

This is precisely what happens with workplace learning and support. The water (content, activities, coaching) exists. It's just too hard to get it to people when and where they need it. We know people are thirsty (knowledge and skills gaps), but we don't know their individual drink preferences or the plumbing isn't in place to deliver a timely beverage. Instead, we firehose everyone once in a while, even though we know they can't consume all of what we send them at one go. Eventually, they go looking for sustenance elsewhere because they find alternative options that meet their tastes.

Content will always be important. L&D will continue building courses, producing videos, and writing assessments. But content cannot be L&D's main focus. We must shift our attention to the learning infrastructure (plumbing) before we think about the content (water). L&D must build a strategy that ensures people have access to right-fit learning and support resources when and where they need help, regardless of the level of disruption or pace of change. We must become organizational plumbers and make sure the necessary pipes (tools, tactics, technologies) are in place and maintained. Sometimes, we'll provide the water that flows through the pipes. More often than not, we'll fade into the background as subject matter experts leverage our learning infrastructure to deliver their own solutions. But we'll always be there to protect the user experience and make sure learning and support are as convenient, timely, and reliable as turning on the faucet.

What should come out of that faucet? It turns out that L&D only does six things.

The Six Things

Every L&D function is different. We work in different industries, support different audiences, have access to different tools, apply different tactics, and abide by different regulations. One team may rely on instructor-led training delivered in classrooms at the home office while another deploys safety training to remote field locations using virtual reality. We do our jobs differently, but everything L&D does can be distilled down to six core concepts (Figure 3-1):

- We provide training on core job knowledge and skills.
- We enable the sharing of accessible, consistent, and reliable information.
- We connect employees to timely, on-demand performance support.
- We provide ongoing practice and reinforcement.
- We support the delivery of personalized coaching and feedback.
- We provide opportunities to explore and develop new skills.

This is more than a list of what L&D does. It's also what every employee needs to do their best work today while developing the skills they'll need to be successful in the future. This list is the tactical side of a modern learning mindset. It's where the rubber meets the road. This is how you close opportunity gaps and foster continuous skill development.

Figure 3-1. The Six Tasks of L&D

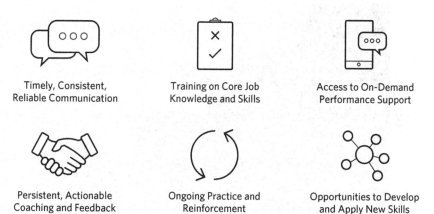

Timely, Consistent, Reliable Communication

Training on Core Job Knowledge and Skills

Access to On-Demand Performance Support

Persistent, Actionable Coaching and Feedback

Ongoing Practice and Reinforcement

Opportunities to Develop and Apply New Skills

L&D sounds pretty simple when you distill it down to six things, right? Well, making these six concepts work is especially challenging if you don't have the right framework in place to guide your strategic L&D decisions. This is true regardless of organization size or complexity. For instance, your team may put most of your resources into training on core job skills but do very little related to reinforcement or performance support. As a result, you may run into problems with knowledge transfer, behavior change, and job execution. To close the gaps and provide equitable support within a constantly changing workplace, L&D must employ a holistic learning strategy. We must bring all the pieces together in a way that makes sense to every stakeholder, especially the people we support.

Building a disruption-ready learning culture starts with a mindset shift. Every stakeholder must agree with and support the role learning plays in helping people keep pace with change. However, to bring this mindset to life with speed and scale, L&D needs a new framework—a model that combines our familiar tools and tactics with proven learning principles.

Creating the MLE Framework

This is it! This entire book exists because of this one image (Figure 3-2). It's not even a fancy image. It's just six bars stacked on top of one another.

Figure 3-2. The MLE Framework

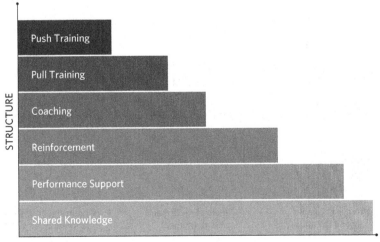

This image demonstrates the limits of my personal design skills. It's also the foundation of my entire philosophy on workplace learning and the tool I use to help organizations around the world rethink their skill development infrastructures. Plus, as I've learned over the past few years, the Modern Learning Ecosystem (MLE) Framework is the commonsense approach many organizations turn to in the face of disruption, whether they know it or not.

I'd love to sit here and claim that, during a moment of unmitigated brilliance, I ran into my office, grabbed a dry erase marker, and diagrammed my vision for the future of workplace learning, but that's not what happened at all. Before you buy into the framework, it's important to discuss how it was developed.

Part 1: Experimentation

I spent six years managing instructional design and learning technology within a contact center operation. I joined the organization during a period of rapid growth. Our parent company had been around for decades, but the digital function in which I worked was still quite new. As a result, they had yet to establish "the way we do things here." This opened the door to a lot of experimentation within L&D. Our "figure it out" mentality was further precipitated by a massive restructuring six months after I was hired. I went from supporting *this many people* (hands held out about six inches apart) to *this many people* (hands spread as wide as they can go) overnight. And I had to do it with fewer resources.

We no longer had the capacity to build online courses to appease every stakeholder request. We weren't permitted to pull people off the contact center floor and into classrooms for training. Agents had to stay on the phone, and we had to figure out new ways to fit learning into their workflow. I tried everything I could think of, and I mean *everything!* Wikis, microlearning, reinforcement, comics, gamification, video practice, and more. I was too inexperienced to know what would and would not work, so I threw everything at the wall to see what would stick. Over time, my team managed to piece together a dynamic learning ecosystem using what would eventually become the MLE Framework.

Part 2: Presentation

I delivered my first-ever conference presentation at about the same time as we were figuring things out within my learning organization. My session was about social learning, one of the many practices we introduced within the contact center during our experimentation phase. I included a slide within my PowerPoint deck that visualized our overall learning strategy. I used simple shapes to show how we stacked all of our tactics—curated content, performance support, formal training, reinforcement, and so on—based on how easy they were to access within the workflow. Remember, I supported contact center agents who were not permitted to leave their desks. This forced me to lean on certain tactics more than others.

It was a visual nightmare of a diagram, but it was also the slide most people took photos of during the session. I soon figured out why.

Part 3: Whiteboardification

I changed jobs two years later. After a month in my role as a learning technology strategist, I was asked to present for a prospective client. The company wanted to modernize their retail learning strategy, and my COO asked me to share my ideas. But there was a problem: I didn't have any ideas! I knew a lot of stuff about workplace learning, but I hadn't had the chance to refine my perspective into something that could be easily shared. So, as I had done so many times before on the job, I winged it.

The night before the meeting I dug through my old industry presentations looking for gems I could use to tell my story. I pulled together a few of my favorite slides, including that ugly ecosystem diagram. The next morning, I spent most of the meeting looking for ways to align my ideas with the ongoing conversation. Suddenly, all the pieces snapped together, and I knew what I was going to do. When it was my turn to speak, I ditched the slides. Instead, I walked up to the whiteboard and drew my version of a right-fit learning ecosystem. I used that ugly slide, which was sitting open on my laptop screen, as a guide. My co-workers watched with blank faces as I diverted from the original plan and outlined a strategy they had never seen before. When I was finished telling my story, I had created the framework that has served as the basis for everything I've done professionally since that day. Bonus: The client loved it!

From Programs to Systems

That's enough of the history lesson. Let's break down the purpose and structure of the MLE Framework before we dig into the details over the next few chapters.

The MLE Framework helps L&D expand beyond our traditional limitations. This is why I use the term *ecosystem* within the name. The framework acknowledges that learning is not based on an individual piece of content or a single event. Rather, a purposeful blend of tools, tactics, and technologies is required to foster ongoing development and performance improvement. The MLE Framework transforms L&D's six core practices into a strategic blueprint.

Think about all of the tactics you currently use to help people learn. Your list may include:

- Classroom training
- Online courses
- Job aids
- Mentoring
- Coaching guides
- Simulations
- Role plays
- Job shadowing
- Games
- Social media
- Videos

How do these tactics fit together as part of a consistent strategy? How do you know when to use each tactic for maximum effect? Too often, L&D tactics are chosen based on convenience or stakeholder requirement, without consideration for what best fits the problem we're trying to solve.

This causes confusion for employees, who are provided with an inconsistent learning experience, and ultimately reduces L&D's effectiveness.

The MLE Framework fixes this problem by aligning our tactics with our core practices. For example, classroom training is a type of push or pull training, while job aids are a form of shared knowledge:

- We provide training on core job knowledge and skills **(push training)**.
- We enable the sharing of accessible, consistent, and reliable information **(shared knowledge)**.
- We connect employees to timely, on-demand performance support **(performance support)**.
- We provide ongoing practice and reinforcement **(reinforcement)**.
- We support the delivery of personalized coaching and feedback **(coaching)**.
- We provide opportunities to explore and develop new skills **(pull training)**.

Each core practice is represented in a layer within the framework. The tactics associated with each practice fit within the matching layers (Figure 3-3).

Figure 3-3. The Layers of L&D Practice

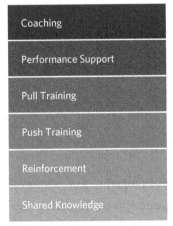

Layers? Tactics? Practices? I admit this can be a bit difficult to follow in written form. So let's do some in-book drawing! Grab a pencil if you're reading the print version. If you're reading the digital version, you'll need a pencil and some paper.

First, use the empty space in Figure 3-4 to redraw the six layers from the last picture. However, draw them based on how you apply them within your organization today. Put the layer you rely on most at the bottom of your stack. For example, if most of your L&D capacity goes toward building e-learning for onboarding and other core job skill training, put push training at the bottom. Then, add the layer you rely on the second-most on top of that. Continue until you've stacked all six layers based on their order of strategic prioritization for your L&D function. When you're done, you'll have built your "House of L&D." Most L&D teams I've worked with draw something like Figure 3-5.

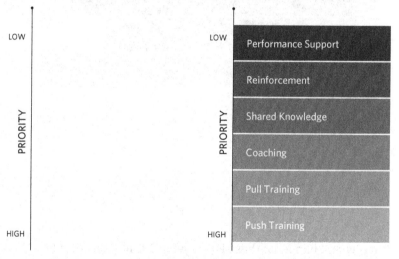

Figure 3-4. My House of L&D   **Figure 3-5.** Common House of L&D stack

The House of L&D is almost always held up by push training—the structured, formal, programmatic stuff. This means employees are expected to set time aside and step away from work to learn on a regular basis. The other layers may show up once in a while, but push training is where most solutions begin.

Many L&D strategies are built from an L&D perspective. Practices and tactics are prioritized based on what works best for L&D, not the audience. Remember, the biggest obstacle to workplace learning is the lack of available time. L&D must consider this factor—availability—as we rebuild our house.

Let's do this by putting our framework layers on an X-Y axis. We've already plotted the Y axis based on prioritization, with the most important layers at the bottom and the least at the top. Now, let's change the length of each layer along the X axis based on availability—how easy or difficult it is for employees to access tactics within each layer. The harder it is to access, the shorter the layer.

Now our picture looks something like Figure 3-6.

Figure 3-6. L&D Practices by Priority and Availability

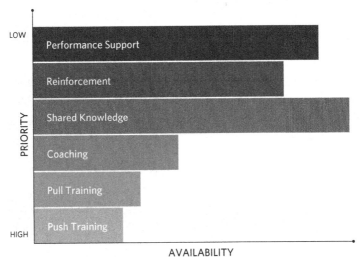

What would happen if these layers were 3-D blocks? Jenga!

The stack would collapse, leaving only the bottom layer or two in place. The same thing happens in workplace learning. L&D may experiment with new layers and tactics now and then. However, when stakeholders continue to ask for two-hour classroom sessions and 45-minute online courses, we ultimately return to our foundational tactics. Our processes default to push training even though it's the least available layer for our audiences. As a result, engagement declines, people must be chased down to complete required training, and the value of L&D routinely gets brought into question.

What if we reorganize the stack from the audience's perspective? What if we put availability first, before we consider our own preferences? Now the picture looks like Figure 3-7.

Figure 3-7. L&D From an Audience Perspective

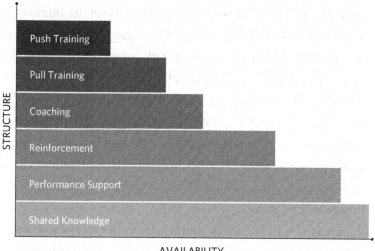

This simple rearrangement transforms the entire learning ecosystem. The MLE Framework puts the employee at the center of the learning experience and overcomes the challenge of time to fit learning into the daily workflow. Because formal training is a last resort rather than a default solution, L&D can deliver right-fit solutions more quickly while providing a support experience that keeps pace with workplace change. The framework's systematic nature ensures a more consistent, seamless, and scalable learning experience for your audiences. Plus, when you integrate each layer within the stacked framework to create blended solutions, every tactic becomes more impactful.

The Person in the Chair

L&D has been trying to make workplace learning less structured and more informal for years. We've long discussed topics like self-directed learning, social learning, and user-generated content. We've come up with snappy catchphrases like "from sage on the stage to guide on the side." But compliance training still needs to get done. Stakeholders still ask for courses. Employees still look elsewhere for help. L&D needs more than a catchphrase. We need an entirely new perspective. This is where the MLE Framework comes in.

Instead of a "guide on the side," the MLE Framework turns L&D into "the person in the chair." It helps L&D pros architect the infrastructure needed to push the right solutions to the right people. More importantly, it helps L&D step aside so the people with information (stakeholders, SMEs) can connect more directly with the people who need it. It finally gets us off the stage by reminding us that L&D was never supposed to be the hero of our own story. Our job is to build heroes. We're not Batman. We're Alfred. We do our best work when no one has to call for help. People may not know we're involved, but we're always there, in the background, making sure Bruce Wayne has the tools he needs to be the best caped crusader he can be.

As you can see, the MLE Framework does not replace your existing learning tactics. Adopting this approach doesn't mean throwing away the great work you've already done. Instead, the framework transforms your existing tactics into a repeatable, scalable system embedded within the flow of work. It makes your organization more agile and proactive. It makes sure the water always flows to the areas where it's needed the most.

Now, let's dig into the MLE Framework layer by layer.

Chapter 4

Layer 1: Shared Knowledge

Transform the Wisdom of the Crowd
Into a Tangible Asset

We're going to dig into the first layer of the MLE Framework: shared knowledge. The tactics within this layer are going to act as the basis for the entire learning ecosystem moving forward, so it's kind of a big deal. We're going to talk about:

- The story of how I discovered the critical importance of shared knowledge in workplace learning
- The benefits of shared knowledge within a modern learning ecosystem
- How to get the right people to share their knowledge
- Why every company needs a curator to make shared knowledge work at scale

I think we have a problem.

Our lead e-learning developer quit the day after I joined the contact center training team. I still don't think it was my fault, but who knows?

His departure meant I was now an e-learning developer. I'd built hundreds of PowerPoint presentations. I'd hacked together a few websites. I was pretty nifty with SharePoint. But I'd never built anything you could really call online training. So, I had to upskill ASAP to keep his projects moving!

While I learned Captivate on the fly, I quickly found that I didn't have all the source information needed to build the first course that would be due. I went hunting on the company intranet. After hours of searching, I couldn't find anything even close to what I needed despite my full access via my L&D credentials.

At first, I thought it was me. I was new. Maybe I just didn't know where to look? I walked around the contact center and asked a few agents I'd met during onboarding how they found information on the job. Their answers confused me even more. One agent showed me a complex hierarchy of folders on his desktop. Another pointed to a shared drive that only certain people could access. Then someone demonstrated how to click click click click click click click through the team SharePoint to find a PowerPoint deck with the information from a meeting that had occurred last quarter. All the while, I was thinking "uh oh . . ."

Armed with these observations, I walked into my boss's office and said, "I think we have a problem." How much time was being wasted by people looking for information every day? How much outdated information was being passed on to customers due to outdated materials being stored on local drives? What if stakeholders were coming to us for so much training because people just couldn't find the information they needed to solve problems on their own?

And then I said the words that changed the trajectory of my career: "What if we built Wikipedia, but for here?"

My boss agreed that we had an information problem. However, we also had a long list of training projects that took priority. This conversation would have to wait. She wrote "Wikipedia" on a sticky note and stuck it on the side of her computer monitor.

That note sat untouched for two years.

Twenty-four months later, my L&D team was asked to consolidate our contact center scripts into a single reference document. I didn't like the idea of creating or maintaining a giant PDF, but that's what our stakeholders asked for. I went along with the concept because I thought this would be my chance to go after the real problem—helping people find information to solve problems in the workflow.

Surprise! The PDF didn't work out. It was too big and hard to use. But agents still needed a way to find all this information on demand.

I jumped at the chance to help my stakeholder find an alternative solution. We met with folks in marketing, who mentioned a wiki platform called Confluence. Then, we chatted with IT, who happened to have an unused license for the same wiki platform. Turns out we had the solution to the problem all along and just never bothered to ask the right people!

My team spent three months setting up a pilot of a wiki-based shared knowledge base. We spent most of that time writing the first 500 articles. We knew we couldn't cover everything from the start. Instead, we spoke with agents to come up with a list of the most highly valued topics—the stuff they used consistently on the job. Then, we partnered with subject matter experts across the product, compliance, and marketing teams to build the pilot content. When everything was ready, we made the wiki available to one team. Within weeks, stakeholders were popping up from every part of the business asking us to add their information to the wiki. Managers were already complaining about the fact that their teams didn't have access yet. It was working!

The wiki had some basic reporting capability, but it didn't offer much insight into how people were using it. So, we plugged it into Google Analytics (for free). I wanted to see the broader picture. What were people searching for? Which resources did they have a difficult time finding? Should the most popular pages be the most popular pages? We used this data along with user feedback to proactively add and revise content. We hit 1 million pageviews in seven months with less than 1,000 users. Three years later, our curator, Sandy, was managing a knowledge base with more than 70,000 content objects and 10,000 users.

Sandy's job was to keep the technology running, enable more than 300 contributors from across the organization, and ensure a consistent user experience. Our contributors included product owners, marketers, managers, and frontline agents—people with the insight and motivation needed to keep our knowledge base up to date. L&D maintained the platform, but the contributors did the real work.

The wiki became the foundation of our workplace learning strategy. Every training request started with the question "What information is available in the wiki on this topic?" If we could solve the problem by writing or updating an article, that's all we did. Formal training requests subsequently dropped by almost 50 percent. Classroom trainers reskilled as they spent more time sharing their knowledge via on-demand content. The LMS took a backseat to the knowledge base, and employees took greater control over their own learning and problem solving.

The wiki was a combination of familiar content and technologies. We borrowed from Wikipedia, YouTube, and Facebook to build a better version of an intranet. We succeeded where SharePoint, Google+, and Yammer had failed. Rather than focus on technology, we leveraged our understanding of digital behavior to help employees use the same habits at work as they did to solve problems at home. The wiki was a huge step forward in reshaping our learning ecosystem, but it was only the beginning.

———

This is the social learning chapter of the book, but it's not called "social learning" because that term is redundant.

Learning is inherently social. People learn from other people. This doesn't always happen during a formal conversation or training activity. You may learn from reading a blog post, watching a YouTube video, or swiping through TikTok. In every case, the information you consume was created by another person. In the cases where content is authored by artificial intelligence, it's still sourced from human insights. Even if you learn how to do something new on your own, you're still building on top of knowledge that was established in collaboration with others. So why do social learning efforts so often fail?

Why Social Tech Fails in the Workplace

The rise of social media during the 2000s and 2010s pushed L&D pros to look for ways to get more people talking within their organizations.

Introducing tools that help people connect and collaborate sounded like a no brainer. Organizations added discussion boards to their SharePoint sites. LMS platforms introduced social features. Yammer brought a Facebook-like experience to the workplace before Facebook launched a product literally called Workplace from Facebook (Meta). But, for the most part, people didn't engage.

L&D has a hard time making social learning work for the same reason we still struggle to take full advantage of smartphones. These world-changing technologies should have prompted us to rethink the fundamentals of how we do our jobs. Instead, we bolted them onto our existing learning strategies. We assumed that, because people share with their friends on Instagram, they'll naturally take advantage of an online discussion board to share knowledge with their co-workers. That hasn't happened. Unfortunately, work is nowhere near as interesting as fantasy football or the new Star Wars TV show.

The problem is our source of inspiration. L&D borrowed from the wrong paradigm when it comes to the connection between sharing and learning. We wanted to be Facebook and Twitter, but the information shared on these platforms is timely and fleeting. We see today, within organizations that use tools like Microsoft Teams, Slack, and WhatsApp, that these platforms facilitate connections and networks between people, but they don't help you codify or discover organizational knowledge. A Slack chat may help you solve your problem right now, but it won't help others solve the same problem in the future. Instead of trying to be Facebook and Twitter, we should have aspired to become Wikipedia and YouTube.

Fixing the Refrigerator

My refrigerator suddenly stopped working a few years ago. It was plugged in, but the light didn't turn on. It also wasn't as cold as usual. I had a freezer full of pizza and chicken that I didn't want to go to waste. That summed up my knowledge of the situation.

How do you think I fixed it?

a) I called a repair person and paid them to fix it.

b) I enrolled in an appliance repair program at a local trade school and fixed it myself three months later.

c) I Googled "refrigerator not working" and watched a YouTube video that explained how to clean the condenser coils.

I chose C. It was the best way to avoid an expensive repair bill and an unnecessary trip to the supermarket. It's also the way we solve most problems in our everyday lives.

We live in a self-service information world. More than 5 billion people around the world have mobile devices (Silver 2019). More than half of the world's population is connected to some form of internet (Clement 2020). "I don't know" is becoming a less and less acceptable answer. If you want to know how old Ted Danson is and you have the means to find out, you can and should know how old Ted Danson is. So, if we solve most of our everyday problems with answers like C, why are companies still basing their learning strategies on B?

Organizations have failed to prioritize shared knowledge (Figure 4-1) within their operational strategies. Some have formal knowledge management practices in place, but the majority leave it up to individual departments. Operations handles the day-to-day. Marketing handles formal communications. L&D handles training. HR handles company-wide policies. IT handles the technology. It's no wonder employees either go looking outside the organization for answers or scrounge together their own resources. Everyone is responsible for their piece of the puzzle, but no one is accountable for the fact that office workers waste almost 10 hours per week hunting for information (IDC 2020). The problem is even worse on the frontline, where only 30 percent of employees in industries like retail, grocery, and contact centers can access information on demand after training (Arlington Research and Axonify 2020).

At home, you can fix a refrigerator on your own in minutes with your smartphone and the internet. At work, the ice cream usually melts before you find the answer.

Figure 4-1. The MLE Level 1: Shared Knowledge

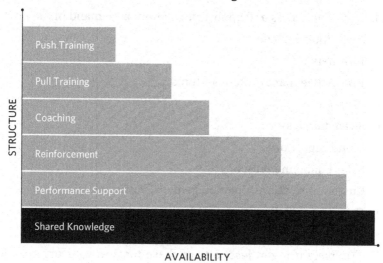

First, Pour the Foundation

Shared knowledge is the foundation of a modern learning ecosystem. It's the layer that makes every other piece—and everything else we'll explore in this book—stronger. It addresses a fundamental workplace reality: People cannot focus on their future skill development needs if they struggle to solve the problems they face every day. But the shared knowledge layer is more than just a static support. It's also an opportunity to curate and disseminate your organization's collective insight. It's a systemic way to avoid the information silos that can stunt an organization's growth, foster employee frustration, and negatively affect performance results.

Pouring the foundation is the first step in building a house. With the MLE Framework as your blueprint, solidifying your shared knowledge approach is the first step to making your learning ecosystem disruption-ready. This layer will serve as the starting point for every L&D initiative moving forward.

This is your "just look it up" layer. It includes all the tools and tactics that help people access and apply information on demand in the flow of work. These tools include:

- Intranets
- Knowledge management systems
- Wikis
- Shared drives
- Cloud repositories
- Sales enablement tools
- Customer relationship management platforms
- Company websites
- Learning content management systems

You're likely using at least one of these tools in your organization right now to store articles, job aids, videos, podcasts, presentations, and more. Or, you may still be relying on antiquated tactics, such as binders and breakroom postings. Regardless of its current state, every organization should begin its learning ecosystem transformation by assessing its shared knowledge capabilities. The goal is to restructure this layer of your ecosystem so information can be accessed, applied, and shared in ways that align with how people do their work.

Shared Knowledge in Real Life: Atlassian

Atlassian has the best technical documentation I've ever seen. This Australian technology company builds software tools for software developers, including Confluence, Jira, and Bitbucket. Their approach to shared knowledge stands out for several reasons:

- Atlassian demonstrates how to build an effective wiki by effectively using their own software product (Confluence).
- The knowledge base is easy to use because it leans into familiar behaviors, such as search and interlinked content. You instinctively know how to use it because you use similar tools online every day.
- Articles are written to help people solve common problems, not learn everything about a topic.

- Users can ask questions and start conversations on a page to get additional support or share their personal insights on the topic.

Check out Support.Atlassian.com to see how you can borrow from Atlassian's approach to building shared knowledge for their customer community.

Benefits of Shared Knowledge

Making information available on-demand may sound like a common-sense part of a learning ecosystem. In practice, building a shared knowledge foundation brings a laundry list of benefits to a workplace learning culture.

Free Information From Format Jail

There's plenty of great information floating around your organization right now. Unfortunately, a lot of it is locked in "format jail"—the information was created in a specific format to meet a particular purpose. For example, product information is presented during a project meeting using PowerPoint. The slide deck then gets distributed across the company and stored for reference in the team SharePoint. However, the format (presentation) no longer matches the use case (problem solving). This makes the information hard to find and apply, especially for audiences who may not be able to easily view the format on their available devices. By prioritizing shared knowledge, you can release great information from incarceration and make it easier to reference in the moment of need.

Make Solutions Available 24/7

Unlike traditional training, shared knowledge solutions are available on-demand within the workflow. People can feed their curiosity and take ownership by solving problems on their own. A well-designed shared knowledge solution lowers the bar for engagement by leveraging familiar behaviors, such as search, interlinked content and social mentions. However, L&D shouldn't just copy and paste from popular social media platforms. Instead, you should apply solutions that align with your audience's needs, fit within their workflows, and apply familiar user behaviors.

Accelerate Problem Solving

Shared knowledge tactics accelerate the solution-making process for users and creators. Problems don't wait for L&D to execute an instructional design process. The workplace is constantly changing, and people need help ASAP. An ID can write an article a lot faster than they can build a course. Shared knowledge channels introduce the option for iterative support. Rather than wait for every detail to be confirmed, contributors can push out information as it becomes available and continue to provide updates as situations evolve.

Shift Accountability From L&D to People Who Do the Work

Your shared knowledge layer is the first step in shifting L&D away from its role as a "knowledge middleperson." With a programmatic approach to learning, L&D sits between SMEs (people who know) and the audience (people who need). It's then our job to build training that pushes SME knowledge to the people doing the work. This slows the flow of information and puts additional accountability onto L&D when we actually have very little to do with the information and how it will be used. Plus, L&D can only handle so many projects with our limited resources. This leads to inconsistency in the workplace support experience, as some topics are given the full L&D treatment while others are shared in less formal ways. A modern shared knowledge strategy connects SMEs directly with users, thereby shifting accountability for learning onto those doing the work. Rather than always building the solution, L&D can focus on activating and maintaining right-fit channels for knowledge sharing. Then, we can prioritize our unique skills and limited capacity on problems that require more complex, structured, programmatic solutions.

Shared Knowledge Considerations

Shared knowledge sounds great, right? It's a powerful practice, but it's also a complicated one. Here are some key factors you must consider before implementing a shared knowledge strategy in your workplace.

Who Is Responsible for Knowledge Management?

There's a fundamental problem with basing your learning ecosystem on shared knowledge: L&D may not own knowledge management practices within your organization. Right now, no one may be responsible for knowledge sharing, meaning L&D can step into the vacuum and help make this an organizational priority for the first time. Or there may be a dedicated team outside L&D that oversees these types of tactics, systems, processes, and content. L&D may be a contributor within these systems but not have the authority to make strategic decisions regarding how they are applied.

This lack of ownership should not deter L&D from starting their ecosystem architecture with shared knowledge. The concept is vital to people's ability to solve problems, regardless of who oversees it. L&D must partner with stakeholders to help them understand the importance of shared knowledge, the role it plays in enabling performance, and how it connects to an organization's learning strategy. From there, L&D may take an advisory or collaborative approach to informing future knowledge sharing strategies so they align with the overall ecosystem architect.

Can You Ensure Right-Fit Access?

Next, you must consider your audience. L&D may support a wide variety of groups that perform very different types of work. Your audience makeup (also known as personas, as we'll explore later) will influence both the types of information they need as well as how they access it. SharePoint may be a great solution for an office-based employee who uses a desktop computer all day, but does it also work for a retail associate who uses a smartphone to do their job on the sales floor? Everyone needs and deserves equitable shared knowledge access. Before you build solutions or choose tactics, make sure you understand your audience's context, especially how they access and use information within the workflow.

Are You Ready to Prioritize Shared Knowledge?

Shared knowledge requires a shift in L&D prioritization. If this layer is meant to act as your strategic foundation, you need to change how you work to make it your strategic foundation. This may mean new processes, systems, technology, content, and so on. L&D is usually overloaded with training requests, and the problems aren't going to stop so you can dedicate time and resources to your transformation efforts. This is where you must balance your grand, long-term vision with short-term gains. Make small, iterative changes to your processes. Add shared knowledge components to your existing solutions so people get a feel for the different ways you can help them address performance challenges. Experiment with new technologies before pushing for wide-scale roll-outs, as I did with my contact center wiki. Make decisions based on your long-term plan, but prove the value of shared knowledge in small bites.

Are You Willing to Delegate Content Development?

Delegation is essential for making this layer work. A shared knowledge strategy cannot scale if L&D is responsible for building and maintaining all the content along with maintaining the delivery channels. There's an infinite amount of potential knowledge within your organization, and L&D only has so many hands available to codify it. Until AI can do all your content creation work for you, you're going to need help. L&D must activate SMEs across the organization as core knowledge contributors. In addition, a curator is going to play an essential role in your knowledge sharing strategy. Contributors can come from any level within the organization. They just need to possess information of value, the willingness to share, and the ability to make sharing part of their job.

These quick-hitting considerations can help get you thinking about shared knowledge. But before you can start building this layer in your learning ecosystem, let's spend extra time on how to get people involved in sharing and who will help curate the content.

Overcoming Disruption With Shared Knowledge

The good news is 98 percent of frontline employees received some type of communication from their employers during the early stages of the COVID-19 pandemic (Arlington Research and Axonify 2020). The bad news is:

- 46 percent found it relevant.
- 40 percent found it reliable.
- 39 percent found it timely.

Shared knowledge strategy does not solve for the lack of information. There's always plenty flying around within the organization. Instead, it addresses the lack of relevant, reliable, timely information, especially during times of significant change. It provides people with a consistent place to go for the latest update and makes them less likely to rely on rumors and hearsay.

Great on-the-job performance starts with awareness. If people do not know, they cannot do. This runs a bit counter to popular L&D arguments that communication and learning are two separate things. True, they aren't the same thing, but they are part of the same overall process. Both concepts enable behavior change. Communication is more perishable while learning is more durable. The right tactics from within the MLE Framework must be applied to the right topics to achieve sustained behavior change and performance results.

Getting People to Want to Solve and Share

Rule 1 of shared knowledge strategy: People need to share for it to work. This chapter began by highlighting how difficult it has been for L&D to get people engaged in social activities. How is this approach going to yield better engagement? Well, there's one huge difference between the stuff we're talking about here and what L&D has tried with social learning:

This isn't about learning!

The foundational layers of the MLE Framework focus on solving problems. This is an operational idea, not a learning one. Yes, people learn so they can solve problems. Yes, solving problems helps them learn through experience. However, the idea that making information more readily available helps people solve problems is much easier to get people to buy into. In fact, many stakeholders already agree with this. They just need help making it happen in ways that don't disrupt the operation.

Let's be honest: People can solve lots of problems without formal training. L&D, along with our stakeholders, has established an unfortunate spoon-feeding habit within workplace learning by limiting people's access to resources. They were hired to do the job. They're trusted to do the job. Plus, they manage to get to work every day on their own. People are fully capable of solving problems—when they're provided with the right resources.

That said, L&D must confront another unfortunate realization. If you provided people with the most comprehensive, easy-to-use shared knowledge solution ever imagined, they probably wouldn't use it—at least not right away. They've spent their entire careers to this point—weeks, months, decades—hunting for information across inconsistent and unreliable sources. They've made "ask the person next to me" the default setting because they trust it more than their other options. Providing a right-fit solution isn't enough. L&D must introduce motivational tactics to shift people's information habits and activate their Google reflexes. This may include:

- Targeted communication campaigns to make sure everyone is aware of the new or revised solution
- Storytelling sessions during which people who have already used and benefited from the solution share their experiences
- Game mechanics to recognize and reward users for engaging with content in desirable ways
- Awareness campaigns to help managers understand the resources available so they can make recommendations during their coaching conversations and team meetings

Ultimately, the best motivator is value. People need to know they will find reliable, up-to-date information every time they use your solution. L&D must make sure their solutions help people solve real problems so they can do their jobs better. This is what changes habits and brings people back. If you spend a lot of time telling people how useful your solution is and they're disappointed during their first use, they probably won't come back.

Now let's talk about how you get people to share. As we already said, shared knowledge strategy doesn't work unless people continuously share. We need the same people who never posted on the discussion board or commented in Yammer to contribute their tacit knowledge in support of the community. To make this work, we must rethink what share means within our organizations.

Let's Be Realistic About Sharing

The internet functions based on the 1 percent rule (Wikipedia 2021), but don't worry about the inexact math. Generally speaking:

- 1 percent of users actively contribute new information to a site like Wikipedia.
- 9 percent engage in ways that help maintain the community (suggesting edits, pointing out errors, making comments, and so on).
- 90 percent benefit from the shared information but do not actively contribute (lurkers).

This is what L&D should expect when it comes to shared knowledge solutions. Employees will not engage equally, but we also don't need them to. Some people possess knowledge on specific topics and will engage more proactively in these areas. Some will just show up, find what they need, and leave. You can't force people to contribute unless it is a defined part of their jobs. For most people, it's just not a priority. Plus, imagine if everyone in your organization shared their latest insights all the time. It's very unlikely that this volume of content would be useful, yet alone manageable or consumable. L&D needs the right people sharing in the right ways at the right times.

So who makes up your 1 percent? Designated SMEs, such as product owners, are used to sharing their knowledge as part of their jobs. This is a great place to start when building a team of champions for your knowledge sharing strategy. Next, find the go-to people within the operation. I'm not talking about "top performers" or the manager's favorite team members. I want the person who always puts together the really ugly PowerPoint slides and forwards them to all of their peers, who then print them out and post them on their cubicle walls because they're so useful. L&D must activate these knowledge leaders to make their contributions formal, scalable, and appreciated. Lastly, consider the role L&D should play as contributors. Your main focus should be establishing channels and building right-fit shared knowledge experiences for end users. However, your team likely possesses considerable operational knowledge based on their past experience and ongoing work. Look for ways to embed sharing into the L&D workflow based on the unique insights available within your own function, including information related to learning and development topics.

Install a Curator

The last piece of the shared knowledge puzzle is the most important. Someone must be responsible for administering your reimagined strategy. Shared knowledge will not work if "everyone" is responsible for sharing. When everyone is responsible, no one is accountable. Every company needs a curator.

The curator does not build every piece of content. Instead, they enable your contributors and maintain the organization's shared knowledge experience. Their only goal is to make sure every employee can access and apply the information they need when and where they need it. In a perfect world, this person actually wouldn't be part of L&D. Instead, they would report directly to senior management to make sure knowledge sharing is a constant priority rather than a departmental project. This shifts shared knowledge from "a learning thing" to an operational necessity. The curator should work alongside IT, communications, marketing, and HR to help align and enable their processes, which will play a critical role in the shared knowledge experience.

The curator must be passionate about documentation. They can close unseen gaps and build resources that benefit the entire organization. For example, how many companies take the time to build their own glossary—a collection of their own unique terminology? This type of resource is particularly helpful for new employees who can't keep up with all the abbreviations and company-speak used in conversations during their first few weeks on the job. The curator will autonomously go after these kinds of issues and solve problems that are rarely prioritized in the short term but affect everyone in the long run. They will also ensure a consistent user experience and finally solve the "where do I go to find" problem that plagues even the most tech-savvy organizations.

The curator will also inform strategic decisions regarding technology. Not to vilify any one department, but the people who buy the tools are rarely the people who use the tools. The curator sets standards for the curation and information sharing. They are a key voice during the procurement of new systems. They also leverage data to assess, validate, and suggest adjustments to your workplace learning strategy. Their insights into how people are using shared knowledge resources, including data points like common search terms and popular topics, will help you identify areas that require more structured training programs.

Start Building Your Shared Knowledge Layer

We've covered why it's a good idea. We've talked about the potential challenges. We've established the job description for your new curator position. Now, let's address how you can get started making shared knowledge the foundation of your learning ecosystem.

1. **Install a curator.** For all the reasons we just explored, this is where you should begin if you want to get shared knowledge right.

2. **Assess your current shared knowledge practices.** Talk to employees, stakeholders, and subject matter experts. Explore how information moves through your organization,

from experts to users. Determine if and how people find the information they need to solve problems on-demand in the flow of work. Spot the gaps.

3. **Evaluate your existing technologies.** Play with every application and device that may enable knowledge sharing. Which ones work, and which leave something to be desired? Make a list of your existing options along with functional gaps that may need to be addressed moving forward.

4. **Run small experiments.** Try new ideas on a small scale. Use your existing tools in different ways to solve shared knowledge problems. See what works and what fails. Validate your understanding of the shared knowledge needs of your audiences.

5. **Engage key partners.** Find your SMEs. Designate your champions. Get IT, legal, HR, and compliance involved early. Make sure your audiences play a key role in shaping your strategy.

6. **Design the shared knowledge experience.** Use everything you've learned so far to outline a right-fit shared knowledge experience for your audiences. Determine how resources will be designed and shared based on user needs. Clarify technology requirements and access points within the workflow. Demonstrate how employees will use your shared knowledge solution to solve problems and improve their performance.

7. **Close strategic gaps.** Document proven processes. Establish a governance model that clarifies how sharing works, based on the requirements within your organization. Assign roles related to administration, review, approval, and maintenance. Acquire new tools if needed.

8. **Determine measurement strategy.** Identify the quantitative and qualitative data you'll need for implementation and ongoing assessment. Socialize your measurement strategy with key stakeholders so they understand what will and will not be tracked and how insights will be used to inform ongoing efforts.

9. **Refine the learning solution process.** Align your L&D processes with your shared knowledge practices. Integrate all

available layers and tactics from the MLE Framework into your solution design.

10. **Apply. Measure. Iterate.** Implement your shared knowledge practices with an initial audience. Analyze and report results from ongoing measurement based on established benchmarks. Iterate your solution based on qualitative feedback and quantitative observations.

11. **Scale.** When this transformation works, every team is going to want in on it. Always make decisions at an enterprise level rather than focusing on just the first few audiences. Be ready to expand your shared knowledge practices across the organization. Make every strategic decision as if it will affect everyone you support.

Last Point

This is one of the longest chapters in the book because it's the foundation of everything you'll do moving forward when applying the MLE Framework. A solid shared knowledge layer will change how you solve problems, how you engage with stakeholders, and how people take ownership of their own learning practices. When SMEs come to you asking for the same old training to solve a new performance problem, you can confidently respond with the same question every time:

> What information is already available on this topic for people who encounter this problem?

If they respond with "nothing," you know where to start!

Chapter 5

Layer 2: Performance Support

Make Sure Everyone Knows How to Raise Their Hands

SPOILER ALERT

We're going to loop performance support into the MLE Framework as the second-most important layer. There's already plenty of great insight in the profession on this topic, but we're going to demonstrate how it fits within the larger picture of the modern learning ecosystem. Let's talk about:

- The benefits of systematic performance support
- What to consider as you increase your reliance on performance support
- The steps to making performance support the second most important part of your learning strategy

What if L&D didn't exist?

If an employee on the third floor of an office building in Phoenix, Arizona, has a question and another employee working from home in Orlando, Florida, has the answer, what can L&D do to help them find each other without having to be responsible for answering the question themselves?

I posed this query to my team in the aftermath of yet another lay-off. I'm sorry, "involuntary resource action." We were now a team of 40 people supporting 10,000 employees located in offices across the country. We had stakeholders coming at us from all directions requesting training on products, processes, regulations, leadership, and more. Our programmatic approach to learning was no longer feasible. We just didn't have the time or capacity to build a course or facilitate a program to solve every problem. We had to find a new strategy that aligned with our changing workplace reality. Senior L&D management held a planning session, and I managed to make everyone mad within the first 10 minutes.

I decided to challenge my peer group to throw out our existing playbook and start from scratch. I asked them, "What would actually happen if L&D didn't exist at all?" What would the company do without a formal learning function? Would they just stop trying to solve performance problems, or would they adapt and find new methods? How could those methods inform our reimagined strategy and make us more agile and proactive?

The pushback was fast and furious. Admittedly, I may not have approached the subject in the best way possible. My "What if we didn't exist" question came across as a judgment "The work we do doesn't matter and people don't really need us." Whoops!

After a while, we managed to overcome our legacy mindset and started thinking more broadly about problem solving without formal training. "If you don't know the answer, can't find the information you need on your own, and don't have the option to attend a training program, what do you do?" As if rehearsed, everyone in the planning session responded in unison: "Ask the person next to you."

But what do you do if the person next to you is just as clueless as you are?

We needed a way to apply the "ask the person next to you" behavior, while making sure that person always had the right answer. We needed to scale it to 10,000 people while covering every possible workplace topic. And we needed to do it fast with almost no budget.

We looked to our everyday lives for inspiration. We discussed technologies like Quora, Reddit, and Facebook. We explored digital communities like Stack Overflow, where credible, like-minded people proactively support one another without the need for formal oversight. Then we looked at our own corporate technology stack to see if we had anything similar that we could try. Turns out, we did.

Enter Google+. Remember that platform? Google was plussing the digital world way before Disney, Apple, and Paramount. Google+ was Alphabet's answer to Facebook and Yammer. It had all your standard social features, like news feeds, groups, mentions, and reactions. Plus (pun intended), it integrated with our core productivity tools like Gmail and Google Drive. Applying it as a performance support tool made total sense. So, we created a few learning-focused communities and gave it a try.

It failed, for all the reasons Google+ failed as a product. Content within this type of social platform is inherently time-bound. If people didn't check it regularly, they had to do a lot of clicking and scrolling to find anything of interest. The platform wasn't a required part of the everyday workflow, so people just kept emailing questions to people who forwarded them to other people who may or may not answer them before going on vacation. My L&D team went back to the performance support drawing board.

The problem was clear: For performance support to work, it had to be directly embedded into the workflow. We took a hard look at the essential tools people used on the job. We discovered the company's knowledge base had a commenting feature. People could add comments to the bottom of an article and get notified via email when someone else responded. This was our best option for giving people the ability to raise their hand within the workflow, so we decided to give it a try. We worked with IT and operations to turn on comments for a small group of product and process articles. We assigned L&D team members to act as community managers (CMs) and make sure anyone asking questions got an answer as quickly as possible during peak operating hours. Operations let employees know about the new commenting option in a weekly update email, and we waited to see if this would end up being another version of the failed Google+ experiment.

Only a few comments were submitted during the first week. Then a few more showed up the next week. Then more. And more. By the end of the first month, we were fielding dozens of questions every day. Not only were employees looking for help, but they were also challenging established processes in very open and honest ways. Our CMs went to work, tagging subject matter experts in their exchanges to make sure everyone got the information they needed. Then, CMs used the information from comments to update articles and reduce the need for future questions.

The real turning point came early during the second month of our performance support experiment. I usually kept the conversation feed open on the side of my screen while working to make sure CMs were keeping pace with employee needs. We had established an internal service level agreement of five minutes to respond to every question to make sure employees knew they would get prompt support and therefore develop a habit of using this platform. My feed had a predictable flow of user comments followed immediately by CM responses. But this time, I saw something different.

An employee in Phoenix, Arizona, had asked a question about a product. Two minutes later, someone responded with an answer. But it wasn't one of my CMs. It was a random employee from Orlando, Florida. I later confirmed that these two people didn't know one another. The Orlando-based employee simply knew the answer, saw the question in their feed and beat my CM to the punch. I screen captured the exchange and emailed it to my boss with the words "It's working." We phased out the CMs within six months as the employee community became self-sufficient. After a year of experimentation, we found a way to scale the concept of asking the person next to you and embedded real-time performance support within the workflow.

———

The shared knowledge layer of the MLE Framework transforms learning into a resource-based strategy. People can look up the information to solve a problem in the moment of need. Product details. Vacation policies. Standard operating procedures. All of this is covered by a solid shared knowledge strategy.

But what happens when someone can't find the answer? Perhaps they found the information but don't know how to apply it to solve their specific problem. Or maybe they have limited experience with the topic and don't even know which information to seek.

Everyone needs (and deserves) help to do their best work. New hires need dedicated support to grow their knowledge and confidence as they get started on the job. But experienced team members also need support, especially with the pace of change in today's workplace.

Performance support is the "I need help" layer of the MLE Framework (Figure 5-1). It's the part of your learning strategy that ensures people's capabilities are not limited to how much the person working next to them happens to know. It's a required component of a modern workplace learning ecosystem because it reduces the risk created when people make guesses because they don't know the correct answers.

Figure 5-1. Performance Support Layer of the MLE Framework

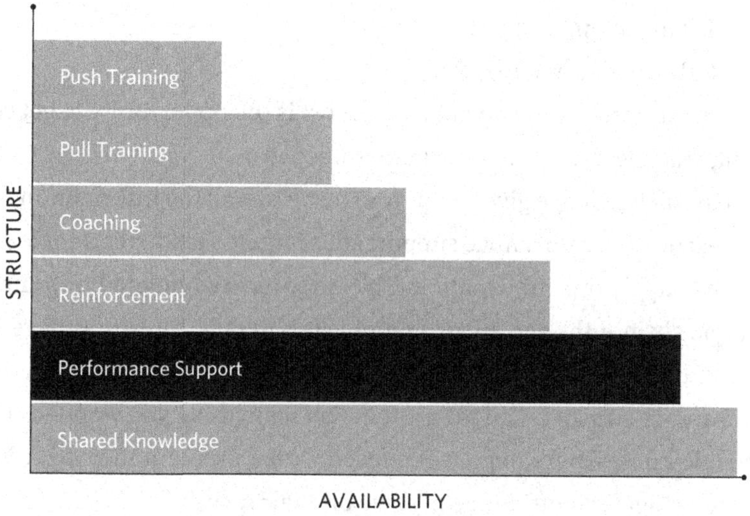

Let's Define Performance Support

Lots of L&D pros know about and already apply performance support. In fact, the concept is almost a victim of its own popularity. If you Google "performance support," you'll quickly realize we don't have an industry-standard definition for it. People spend a lot of time discussing what does and does not constitute performance support rather than focusing on solving the problem. In the end, the practice is infinitely more important than the term. Nonetheless, here's the current entry from the Association for Talent Development's online glossary:

> *Performance support provides just enough information to complete a task when and where a performer needs it. The support is embedded within the natural workflow and is organized for use within a specific context, such as the location or role that requires completion.*

There's an ever-growing list of tactics that can be used to support performance within the moment of need, including:

- Checklists
- Question and answer forums
- Chat tools and bots
- Digital adoption platforms
- Subject matter experts

The bottom line: Performance support is the opportunity to get consistent, reliable help whenever help is needed.

Shared knowledge gives employees access to all the information they may ever need. Performance support adds targeted guidance people may require to apply this information. They may have completed training on the topic six months ago and forgotten a few details. They may have discovered the topic independently and not know how to apply it. Call it performance support. Call it a crutch. Call it anything you want—as long as people know where to go when faced with a problem they don't have the knowledge or confidence to solve on their own.

I'm writing one chapter on performance support. I certainly did not create the concept. The topic has been explored in great detail by super smart L&D professionals over the past 20 years, including these:

- Bob Mosher and Conrad Gottfredson literally wrote the book on this concept in 2010 with *Innovative Performance Support: Strategies and Practices for Learning in the Workflow.*

- Guy Wallace (currently president at EPPIC Inc.) has done a lot of great work to help organizations shift their focus from learning to performance enablement.
- Sebastian Tindell (currently head of learning and development operations at Vitality) has a great perspective on applying a resource-based approach to learning.
- Marc Rosenberg helped me recognize the connection between knowledge management and performance support with his 2005 book *Beyond E-Learning: Approaches and Technologies to Enhance Organizational Knowledge, Learning, and Performance.*
- Shannon Tipton (currently the chief learning officer at Learning Rebels) blends the concepts of performance support and microlearning in her practices.

Check out these folks if you want to dive deep into all things performance support. This concept is often discussed from a tactical perspective by showcasing the ways L&D can create performance support tools. The MLE Framework goes a step further by taking a systems approach to make performance support an integrated part of the workplace experience. It's not a question of if you provide performance support. It's a question of how you make sure people always have access to it, regardless of role, location, experience, or topic.

Performance Support in Real Life: Google Maps

When's the last time you used a map? A standard, paper, oh my gosh how do you possibly fold this back into a shape that fits in the glove compartment map? That map would be an example of shared knowledge. A cartographer documented their knowledge of a geographic region into a shareable format. The information is available for you to use within the context of performing a task—by fitting into the glove compartment of your car. However, the map itself is flat. It can't proactively guide you to your destination or adapt to your needs.

Google Maps may be the best example of everyday performance support. Yes, it's a map. But it's a map that actively pushes you in the right direction to achieve your goal. It provides you with options and details about your journey. It makes suggestions for alternative routes to avoid traffic. It helps you find the nearest Publix when you need to take a restroom break in the middle of your trip.

L&D teams everywhere should reference Google Maps as the model for right-fit performance support.

Benefits of Performance Support

Now that we've established what performance support is and how it relates to shared knowledge, let's explore the benefits your organization can derive by embedding the concept within the foundation of your modern learning strategy.

Accelerate Problem Solving and Time to Contribution

We've already talked about how much time people waste at work looking for information. A shared knowledge strategy makes it easier to find information that has been codified. Performance support fills in the blank when knowledge has not been captured. Instead of wasting time trying to find the right people to answer employee questions, performance support pushes people to the right channels and subject matter experts to get their problems solved ASAP. This is especially important for people who are new to their roles. Organizations can accelerate their onboarding processes by leveraging performance support as a crutch while new hires develop their foundational job knowledge and skills.

Boost Employee Confidence on the Job

Performance support boosts confidence by validating the information used to make decisions in the flow of work. There's a popular statistic floating around online that claims adults make 35,000 decisions a day. However, this poorly cited claim doesn't really line up with common sense. After all, if a person sleeps for eight hours per day, that would mean they make more than 36 decisions per minute. How many decisions have you made since you started reading this paragraph? Unless breathing, blinking, and chewing are decisions, this number probably goes into the same pop science bin as "people have shorter attention spans than goldfish." Nonetheless, people make a lot of decisions on the job, and the persistent opportunity to get help with those decisions can make employees more accurate and confident in their performance.

Leverage Existing Subject Matter Expertise

Like user-generated content, performance support can shift L&D away from its traditional role as knowledge middleperson and directly connect those who know with those who need. Rather than trying to be a SME on every subject, L&D pros can focus on installing and maintaining the channels needed to provide consistent performance support at scale. For example, L&D may set up topical channels in Microsoft Teams or provide templates for operational checklists. SMEs with proven expertise can then step in and share their knowledge directly with employees. L&D rightly takes a back seat, measuring the effectiveness of performance support tactics and making strategic adjustments to improve outcomes. Remember—we're Alfred, not Batman.

Reduce the Need for Formal Training

It's unfair to suggest that everyone can figure out how to execute complex work processes with just shared knowledge resources. Sure, some people may be able to pick things up on their own. But others will benefit from additional help. However, that doesn't necessarily mean they need formal training. They may simply require extra guidance, like a reliable checklist and a go-to person for questions. This is where performance support comes in. As one of the middle layers in the MLE Framework, it provides more structured support than shared knowledge without going so far as to require push training. If people are unable to achieve their performance goals with this level of on-demand support, additional layers and tactics may be required.

Performance Support Considerations

Performance support is another commonsense concept. Who doesn't want to make sure employees can get their questions answered and avoid making risky guesses on the job? That said, it's not always easy to implement reliable performance support tactics, especially within large, distributed organizations. Here are some important questions to ask before constructing your performance support layer.

Are You Sure They Don't Need to Remember This?

Performance support is not designed to help people retain information. It doesn't matter if you're using an electronic performance support system (EPSS) to guide salespeople through the process of adding new opportunities in your CRM or implementing a chat bot to respond to common HR questions. Performance support tools help people do their jobs in the moment. Of course, people may pick up and retain some information long term. But that's not the goal. If you want employees to retain knowledge so they can reliably apply it on the job without help, you'll need to apply tactics from additional MLE Framework layers. More on that in a bit!

Can You Ensure Right-Fit Access?

The ATD definition of *performance support* includes the phrase "embedded within the natural workflow and is organized for use within a specific context." Your performance support channels must fit the day-to-day working realities of your audience. A digital adoption tool may be a useful tactic for remote workers who sit in front of a computer all day, but it may not apply to grocery employees who use limited technology on the job. Each persona within your organization needs performance support they can access without interrupting their workflow (there's that word persona again, more coming on that later). To add seamless, frictionless support within the work experience, you may need to provide different tools for different audiences. Technology may hit the mark for some employees while others may benefit from a low-tech solution. When it comes to learning and performance, one size almost never fits all.

Are People Getting Timely Support?

How long are you willing to wait for an answer you need to solve a problem at work? A week? A day? 14 minutes? It took me three seconds to figure out Lebron James is 6'9" thanks to Google. That's the bar L&D is compared to when it comes to getting people the information they need to do their jobs. Select tactics that provide simple, prompt support. You may need to go so far as providing employees with service level agreements (SLAs) that guarantee the time it will take to get a question answered, thereby demonstrating your commitment to supporting their performance. Make sure you keep your promises and provide the most convenient support possible. Otherwise, people will keep guessing because the risk is less disruptive than your performance support tactics.

Should Your Performance Support Be Active or Passive?

Active performance support pushes unprompted suggestions and guidance to an employee. For example, a tool tip may pop up within a workplace system to walk an employee through a new feature. Passive performance support must be requested by the employee on-demand. A Slack channel where SMEs answer questions about new product releases is a passive tactic. L&D must determine when active or passive tactics best fit their audiences' work context and problem-solving needs. When you mismatch performance support strategies with user needs, you get Clippy—the much maligned Microsoft Office application helper from the 1990s and 2000s. Trust me: No one wants Clippy!

Can You Ensure Consistency and Accuracy?

Not only does performance support need to be fast, it must also be reliable. Employees are putting their performance in your hands by relying on L&D support tools. In some cases, this could mean their personal safety is at risk if performance support is inaccurate. Make sure all performance support tools are continuously maintained just like traditional courses and instructional material. Leverage community managers to keep an eye on social performance support tools, such as chat channels and question and answer forums. Ask employees for feedback regarding their performance support experiences to make sure they're getting the intended value from L&D tactics.

How Committed Are Your Subject Matter Experts?

Subject matter experts often play a critical role in performance support. They may respond directly to employee questions in online forums or provide the content used to create an EPSS guide. In every case, they must understand the context in which their information will be applied and demonstrate ongoing commitment to supporting employee performance. This means extra work. It's important and it adds value, but it's still work. Partner with SMEs who are willing to take this work on and agree to be held accountable for providing timely, up-to-date support. If a SME resigns or transfers, make sure this performance support role is included in their replacement's list of duties.

Overcoming Disruption With Performance Support

"Talk to your manager if you have any questions about this huge change that may or may not impact your life."

Have you heard this one before? A few times? How often can that manager actually answer your questions because they know every detail of what's going on? Not so much.

The opportunity to ask questions and get timely, reliable answers is a fundamental employee right. Unfortunately, it's not always true in today's workplace. More than 65 percent of frontline employees feel well informed about changes that affect them in the workplace, according to *The State of the Frontline Work Experience in 2021 Report* (Arlington Research and Axonify). The pace of change has been accelerated by the COVID-19 pandemic, but companies were already struggling to keep people informed prior to 2020. This fact is echoed in the way performance readiness varies by job status and working location:

- 71.3 percent of full-time employees feel informed about workplace changes, compared with 54 percent of part-time employees.
- 78.7 percent of office-based employees feel informed, compared with 59.5 percent of store or branch-based employees.

Everyone needs and deserves an equitable opportunity to raise their hand and ask for help as their workplaces evolve around them. L&D can help organizations prioritize performance support as part of their change management strategies. We can help our partners move away from the FAQ version of information flow and ensure everyone has a place to go to get their questions answered, regardless of role, status, or location. By embedding performance support tactics within the workflow, L&D can reframe change as something that is done *with* employees, not *to* employees.

Start Building Your Performance Support Layer

Now that we've covered the benefits of performance support and some practical considerations, let's run through the steps to begin adding performance support into your learning ecosystem.

1. **Assess the workflow.** To help people gain access to on-demand support within the workflow, you must understand the workflow. Assess the day-to-day realities for your audiences. Identify potential access points, including hardware and software tools, that may be used to provide performance support.

2. **Identify common struggle points.** Talk to your audience. Find out where they struggle on the job. When do questions tend to pop up? How often are they in need of guidance? How would they prefer to access performance support? Align your performance support tactics with these points of need.

3. **Identify niche use cases.** Find examples where specialized performance support tools may be required. Are there certain processes that consistently require extra guidance? Is this guidance necessary for every employee or only those with less experience? Be ready to build targeted solutions, but only when required.

4. **Clarify retention requirements.** Be sure people can do their jobs effectively with performance support. There are plenty of cases where people are expected to know the answer, and regularly asking for help or leaning on support tools creates an impediment to performance. Make sure performance support is an enhancement, not a replacement for employee capability.

5. **Involve subject matter experts.** Performance support often connects those who know with those who need. Before you put any tactics in place, you need to be sure those who know are on board. Identify potential champions by topic who will act as go-to SMEs within your performance support scheme, especially if L&D will not facilitate the solution directly.

6. **Install hand-raising tactics.** Give people a consistent place to go when they need help. It could be a digital solution or a designated subject matter expert on the team. Make sure your hand-raising tactics fit within your audience's workflow. A chat app is a poor choice for a performance support tool in retail if store associates can't access it while working with customers.

7. **Measure utilization, sentiment, and impact.** Performance support enables execution by improving both knowledge and confidence. People can feel secure in their decision making thanks to the ability to rely on proven expertise, especially if they have limited experience with the topic at hand. This is why it's important to collect a range of metrics to determine the value of a performance support tactic. This includes utilization (are people using it as intended), sentiment (do people find it helpful), and impact (is it leading to improved performance).

Last Point

Shared knowledge and performance support are the two required layers within the MLE solutioning process. No matter what problem you're trying to solve, people need timely access to information and the opportunity to ask for help.

Next, we're going to cross an important line within the MLE Framework. So far, we've been discussing the nice-to-know stuff—the information people can look up while doing their jobs. Now, let's talk about the need-to-know—the knowledge people must retain to do their jobs well.

Chapter 6

Layer 3: Reinforcement

Separate the Need-to-Know From the Nice-to-Know

We're going to talk about the science of learning. Yes, learning is a science. Enabling learning is an art. Get ready for:

- The difference between need-to-know and nice-to-know information at work
- The science of learning reinforcement, including overviews of retrieval practice, spaced learning, interleaving, and metacognition
- The benefits of making reinforcement part of everyday learning
- Essential considerations for introducing reinforcement into the busy workflow
- How to start building a reinforcement layer that works for everyone

You're not going to Hollywood!

I once designed training for *American Idol*. OK—so it wasn't the TV show. It was the theme park attraction at Walt Disney World.

I had made a bit of a name for myself within L&D based on the instructor-led training session I designed for the opening of the Kim Possible World Showcase Adventure at Epcot. Over the course of two hours, cast members learned how to apply Disney service principles while battling a fictional villain who was sneakily ruining guest experiences all over the park. The character was played by a peer of mine who was nice enough to don a cape, fake mustache, and bowler hat during a series of videos that I embedded within the class PowerPoint. The interactive learning experience received rave reviews and got me promoted. I subsequently used the PowerPoint deck as a demo with other teams who asked for guest service training. "We want something like Kim Possible" became a standard request—and a sentence you only hear when you work in L&D at Disney.

The operations team at Disney's Hollywood Studios was weeks away from opening the American Idol Experience. Guests could audition to perform on stage in front of a live audience, just like on the TV show. Operations would be responsible for ushering guests in and out of the audition space as well as the loading the audience in and out of the auditorium where performances took place throughout the day. They heard about the Kim Possible program and wanted one just like it for their new attraction. I gladly obliged.

I worked with the attraction's management to understand guest service expectations within the new location. We walked through the various roles and discussed how cast members could enhance the guest experience during their brief interactions. I then designed a highly themed two-hour training experience. Participants would demonstrate their guest services skills in front of a (pre-recorded) panel of judges during a series of in-class activities. You know—just like on the TV show. Then, before the final performance, everyone would leave the classroom and head to the attraction so participants could rehearse their skills in the physical locations where they'd be applied in real life. Once they were back in the classroom, they'd take part in a final activity. The judges would always love it, of course. Everyone wins in this version of the show!

Once again, people loved the training. I observed the sessions from the back of the room, taking notes and providing feedback to facilitators along the way. During the last class, I was joined by a group of entertainment managers. The operations team would handle guest services at the attraction, but entertainment would step into the judge roles. They would decide who was good enough to progress through the multiple rounds of auditions and ultimately make it onto the big stage for a live performance in front of hundreds of guests. The management group wanted to see if the operations training made sense for their team. When the class ended, they told me they wanted to run additional sessions for their entertainment cast. I said no.

The class was a lot of fun. It was themed to the attraction. It provided practical tips for delivering a great guest service experience. However, the behaviors we focused on during the activity-driven experience were specific to operations roles. They didn't match the job entertainment would be doing within the attraction—auditioning guests. More importantly, the class didn't take into account the biggest obstacle facing the entertainment team, one they may have underestimated to that point. They would have to say no to guests. Of course, people get told no all the time, even when they pay lots of money for a dream Walt Disney World Resort vacation. But this time, cast members would have to tell people they weren't good enough to participate in an attraction—without hurting their feelings or crushing their aspirations. That's a difficult task, and the current class wouldn't help them do it.

Instead, I offered to build a new version of the program focused on the right set of behaviors. Based on what they saw in the operations sessions, management agreed—as long as I could pull it off within two weeks. I huddled with my team to quickly figure out how to train cast members to say no, but in a Disney way. This request was so unique compared to our typical training requests that we decided to approach it from a totally different angle. We couldn't just build a standard class with a few activities. Instead, we would design an immersive simulation. Rather than telling people the right way to say no, we would help them find their own ways through targeted practice.

We worked with entertainment management to understand the American Idol audition process, specifically the guidelines around accepting and rejecting guests for the stage show. My team designed a two-hour facilitated simulation that could be experienced by up to six participants at one time. We hoped to execute the experience in the attraction building where cast members would do their jobs for real, but it wasn't available in time. So, we recreated the space, including an audition room and waiting area, in a backstage classroom. Then, it was time to run the entertainment group through the simulation.

The experience began with a quick debrief on the audition process and cast member expectations. Then, two participants stepped into the roles of host and judge. The host was responsible for helping guests prepare for their auditions and departing afterward. The judge facilitated the audition and provided feedback. The remaining session participants observed the simulation and took notes for later discussion. Three L&D facilitators ran the experience. Two portrayed guests. One was a confident, skilled performer. The other was a nervous, unskilled tourist. The third facilitator managed the entire simulation and kept things moving on a timer. Each round lasted 20 minutes, after which the group sat down to discuss the experience. New participants then rotated into the simulation, and facilitators adjusted the experience to introduce new variables to the scenario.

I won't go into detail on everything that happened during that first session. Let's just say it was the only session we ran. Entertainment management shut the program down to reassess the audition experience. The practice session helped them realize that the job would be more difficult than they initially thought. They ended up reworking parts of the audition process to improve the overall guest experience—all because of our training simulation. If we had just delivered a themed two-hour class, the cast may have run into these problems in real life instead of within the safety of a classroom.

I didn't receive the same rave reviews on this training program as I had with Kim Possible. Instead, the experience helped me recognize the importance of practice in the workplace and how a low-risk environment can help you identify the knowledge and skill that truly makes a difference.

What did you have for lunch last Tuesday?

You may be wondering what this question has to do with L&D. Trust me—it will come in handy in the future. Take a moment to recall what you had to eat on Tuesday. Got it? OK. We'll come back to that later.

People are people. We can only take in and retain so much information, and we know it. That's why it may have taken longer than expected to remember what you had to eat just a few days ago. We're built this way on purpose. It's an evolutionary feature, not a defect. People are wired to remember what matters most. It could be because we use the same knowledge all the time, like how to get home from work. Or it may be due to an emotional connection, like the lyrics to the song your mom sang to you when you were a kid. Regardless, people have limits when it comes to memory, no matter where they work.

Building memory also takes time, especially when it comes to complex subjects. It took me at least 50 viewings to memorize all the dialogue from *Back to the Future*. People need to try, fail, correct, succeed, and repeat over and over to master a new skill. Think about anything you're good at. How long did it take you to get good? I was scared to death of public speaking for the first 18 years of my life. It took years of practice to get to the point where anyone would want to listen to me talk (and I'm still not convinced they really do, but, as George McFly once said, "If you put your mind to it, you can accomplish anything").

Reinforcement is one of the most powerful practices available to L&D to help people build and retain knowledge. Unfortunately, it's also one of the least utilized practices in workplace learning. That's why it gets its own layer within the MLE Framework (Figure 6-1).

Figure 6-1. The Reinforcement Layer of the MLE Framework

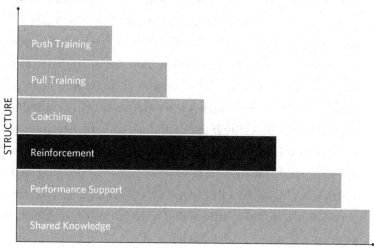

Insert Learning Science Here!

I'm not an expert on the science of learning. I'm a practitioner who's spent years studying insights shared by very smart, uber-qualified people and applying right-fit practices within the frontlines of workplace learning. That said, I have a few science-backed beliefs about learning that inform all my practices:

- Learning is a personal, internal process about which we don't know all that much.
- Learning is not something L&D can create, regardless of how much the term is thrown around and misapplied.
- All learning is self-directed. It's up to the individual to focus their attention and decide to be open to new information.
- L&D can put people in classrooms and push content to their screens, but we can't force them to learn.

These principles are embedded throughout the entire MLE Framework. Reinforcement just happens to be the most science-specific layer. So I figured it's a good spot to address some related information.

I'm going to take a common-sense approach to learning science in this chapter. If you want to dig deeper into the research, here's a short list of resources with tons of references you should check out:

- Everyone in this profession should read *Make It Stick* by Peter Brown, Henry Roediger, and Mark McDaniel. I'm serious. If you're reading my book before *Make It Stick,* you've made a mistake. Stop reading right now. Read that book to get a simple breakdown of what we know about how learning works. Then come back and pick up from this point. Don't worry. I can wait.
- *Design for How People Learn* is the other book everyone in L&D should read, especially if you're an instructional designer or content developer. Julie Dirksen created the ultimate desk reference for how IDs can take advantage of everything we know about learning factors like memory, attention, environment, and motivation to build solutions that have the best possible chance of changing real-world behavior.

- Patti Shank wrote an entire series of books on how to get better learning outcomes from evidence-based principles. *Write Better Multiple-Choice Questions to Assess Learning* is particularly useful within the context of knowledge reinforcement.

- Clark Quinn gets the prize for best book cover in the history of L&D. *Millennials, Goldfish & Other Training Misconceptions* is as fun as it sounds. Clark breaks down a few dozen of the most well-known pop science concepts, including Dale's Cone, neuro-linguistic programming, and learning styles, and explains what the research really says. If you've ever used the term "digital native" as anything other than a punchline, you should read Clark's book.

- Will Thalheimer has done years of amazing work translating scientific research into language that even I can understand. You can find lots of great resources on his website (worklearning.com).

Thankfully, you don't have to be a cognitive psychologist or neuro-scientist to be an effective learning professional. However, you do have to acknowledge and appreciate the realities of our profession. The human brain is infinitely complex, and we don't know much about how it works. Therefore, to get the best possible outcomes, we must take advantage of every trick we've picked up over decades of research. Far too many solutions fail because L&D pros and their stakeholders ignore the common-sense realities of learning.

Up until this point in our story, we've been focused on the nice-to-know side of learning—information people can look up to solve problems and improve their performance. Now, we're shifting to the need-to-know—knowledge people must retain to do their jobs effectively. Luckily, the foundation we've built through shared knowledge and performance support will help us better focus our more structured tactics, starting with reinforcement (Figure 6-2).

Figure 6-2. Reinforcement Separates Need to Know From Nice to Know

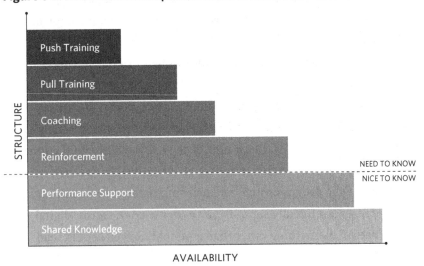

Applying a Need-to-Know Strategy

Still wondering why I asked about lunch on Tuesday?

My boss uses this question to explain the importance of reinforcement. Most people don't remember right away. After connecting a few mental dots, they're able to recall what was previously dismissed as unimportant information. It was back there somewhere, but it wasn't top of mind enough to recall immediately. Luckily, they didn't need to use this information to solve a problem on the job. It's a simple but powerful way to help people acknowledge the limits of human memory and the risk it introduces to the workplace.

Employees are constantly bombarded with a never-ending stream of workplace information. Email. Chat. Customers. Co-workers. Bosses. Meetings. People have great attention spans (way better than a goldfish could ever dream of . . . if goldfish dream), but we often need help focusing on the most important information so we don't get overwhelmed and miss something we'll need to know later.

People begin to forget information almost as soon as the training ends (Figure 6-3). To work within the unavoidable limits of human memory, we must adjust the way we structure L&D solutions.

Figure 6-3. The Forgetting Curve

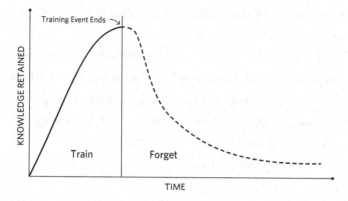

People can look up the vast majority of job information in the moment of need. Grocery cashiers don't have to remember the product codes for every fruit and vegetable in the produce section. They may remember that bananas are #4011 because they ring them up so often, but they can just as easily look up the codes for less popular items like artichokes (#4084). This is why shared knowledge and performance support play such critical roles in establishing the foundation of the learning ecosystem.

Then there's the information people are expected to retain and apply on the job without support. A cashier may be able to look up product codes without slowing their performance, but a deli worker must recall how to safely and effectively operate a meat slicer, which is a dangerous but essential piece of equipment. Performance support can help keep employees safe, especially if they're new to the job. But if employees had to refer to a guide or checklist before serving every customer, the deli line would get a lot longer, and sales would decline precipitously.

Structured training is often the default solution for focusing people's attention and reducing workplace distractions. Spending concentrated time in a classroom or working through an e-learning module can help information pass into working memory. However, if people don't immediately go out and apply what they learned on the job, that information probably won't make it to long-term memory. When it eventually does come time use this knowledge, people will struggle to remember it. This is when people start making guesses or rely on the questionable knowledge of the person working next to them. This is where reinforcement comes in.

A persistent reinforcement strategy embeds meaningful practice within the workflow. It gives people an ongoing opportunity to practice what they've learned and transfer knowledge into performance. Reinforcement can take on many different forms, including:

- Role-play scenarios
- Virtual reality simulations
- Question-based learning
- Reflection activities
- Subscription learning
- Knowledge checks

It's L&D's job to apply the reinforcement tactics that fit into the workflow and provide the best opportunity for people to practice applying their knowledge and skill.

Consider an example. Management wants every salesperson to know the most important details about a new medical device product along with the results of three sample case studies they can cite during their sales calls. L&D hosts a training session on the product for salespeople, where the product manager provides an overview of the device and explains its value to the marketplace. L&D also provides the sales teams with detailed fact sheets (shared knowledge) and a Microsoft Teams channel to ask questions (performance support). However, L&D knows salespeople handle multiple products and therefore cannot predict when they may have their next call about this new device. As a result, they fear people will quickly forget the information provided during the training and be forced to rely on documentation during sales calls, resulting in a lack of confidence and efficiency during these conversations.

Have you ever faced a similar situation? Let's apply the principles of reinforcement to overcome this challenge and ensure the right knowledge is retained long term.

Applying the Principles of Reinforcement

First, L&D must identify the need-to-know information related to the new product, including key specs and case study details. Next, they must determine which reinforcement tactic best fits their sales audience. Salespeople are constantly on the go, traveling to prospect offices and making dozens of calls every day. Plus, they're not exactly known for doing extra tasks unless those tasks directly impact their earning potential. Whatever tactic L&D selects, it must be simple to use, easy to access, require minimal time, and demonstrate a clear impact on sales results.

Reinforcement activities are more effective than simply rereading the product fact sheet before meetings because they apply *retrieval practice,* also known as the testing effect. As the authors of *Make It Stick* put it, "we know from empirical research that practicing retrieval makes learning stick far better than re-exposure to the original material does." Did you use flash cards to prepare for tests in school? It's the same concept. Asking people to recall information strengthens the neural pathways required for knowledge application. This is why older millennials like me remember our home telephone numbers from childhood more than 20 years later. We used the information so much that it became metaphorically burned into our brains.

In this case, L&D decides to use question-based learning to help salespeople retain the right knowledge. They write a series of multiple choice, scenario-based questions that will challenge the salespeople's ability to answer customer questions about the new product. The questions will be pushed to their mobile devices via the LMS. Now L&D must decide when to trigger the reinforcement activity. That's where *spaced learning* comes into play.

Did you ever cram for a final exam? I remember staying up all night and studying for over 10 hours for a high school history test. Yes, I was that kid. I got an A, but I barely remembered anything about the subject a few weeks later. That's the problem with massed practice, according to Patti Shank's research. It's effective in the short-term but fails to trigger long-term retention. Spaced learning involves repeated exposures to small amounts of information over an extended period. Once again, research shows this to be a more effective approach for enabling long-term knowledge retention.

Therefore, L&D takes a technology-enabled approach to support the sales team. They apply their LMS's personalization algorithm to deliver reinforcement questions based on individual salesperson performance. If a salesperson answers questions on a topic correctly, they may not see that topic again for a few weeks. If they answer questions incorrectly, that topic will automatically move to the top of the priority list and reappear more frequently. Based on the amount of content and the desire to fit reinforcement seamlessly within the sales workflow, L&D recommends they complete two five-minute practice sessions per week.

As you can see, retrieval practice and spaced learning are critical elements of an effective reinforcement strategy. They're even more impactful when combined with additional evidence-based principles, such as interleaving and metacognition.

Interleaving involves blending the practice of two or more related topics or skills. Imagine you want to become a great ice hockey player. You'll need a variety of skills, including skating, passing, and shooting. When building your training plan, you shouldn't focus all your practice time on becoming an expert skater before you ever pick up a stick. Instead, you should build a foundation in each basic skill before blending them together in the same way you would during gameplay. That's interleaving in a nutshell.

In our example, L&D introduces questions on additional sales process topics alongside content focused on the new medical device. This helps salespeople practice associated skills—what they're selling and how to sell it—together in the same way they'll apply them on the job.

Metacognition refers to "thinking about thinking." It speaks to our awareness of our own knowledge and how we go about learning and solving problems. The better we grasp our own capabilities, the better we can focus on what matters most when building our skills. It's critical for L&D to help people understand how learning works within the workplace. This means shifting away from a content-centric model and toward applying a consistent and meaningful blend of methods that help people recognize their own development needs.

In our sales example, L&D applies a *confidence-based assessment* within their practice scenarios. Salespeople are asked to select the correct answer to each question. They're also asked to rate their confidence level for their selected answer. This nudges the salesperson to reflect on their knowledge level. It also provides L&D with additional data, as they can compare each salesperson's knowledge and confidence to determine how comfortable they'll be when applying what they've learned on the job.

On the surface, it may seem like L&D's solution to the sales challenge is simple. They just wrote a multiple-choice assessment like they'd do for any other project. However, they didn't just give salespeople a test. They used questions to support learning and retention rather than a one-time assessment. By applying five proven learning science principles to plan and execute this reinforcement strategy, they've increased the chances salespeople will retain the right information long-term, increased the value of the initial training event, and improved the chances the team will meet its performance goals (Figure 6-4).

Figure 6-4. The Forgetting Curve Resolved by Reinforcement Activities

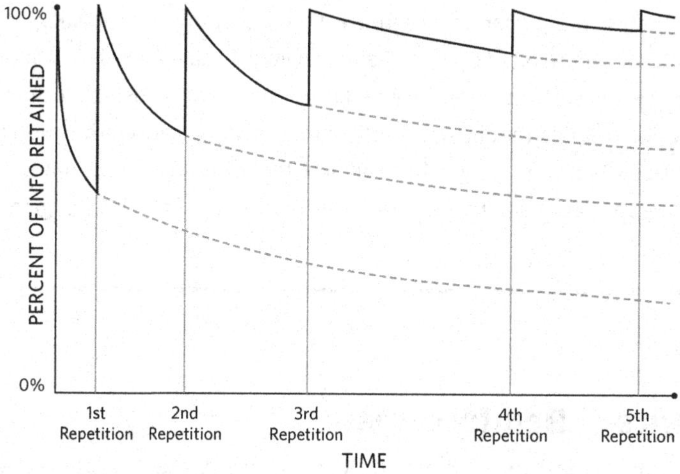

Reinforcement in Real Life: Duolingo

How many times have you heard someone say, "I took four years of [insert language] in high school but can't remember any of it"?

Maybe it's an American thing—only 20 percent of people in the US can converse in more than one language compared with 56 percent of Europeans (CIS 2018). Regardless, language is one of the best examples of how a lack of reinforcement hinders the long-term value of learning.

Picking up a new language is hard. Not only do you have to learn the vocabulary, but there are also factors like cultural context, verb conjugation, written characters, and gender inclusion. Plus, language is application-based. You don't just have to know the words. You have to use them efficiently to communicate your thoughts. If you don't use your new language skills on a regular basis, you end up with a loose memory of catchy phrases like *¿Dónde está la biblioteca?*

If only I had Duolingo in high school! Duolingo is an awesome model for how reinforcement can be applied in workplace learning. Their implicit learning approach focuses on application as opposed to rote memorization. Rather than just explaining concepts, they challenge you to solve problems using written and spoken language and provide immediate feedback. As the studies shared on the "Efficacy" page on their website show, this accelerates the learning process while keeping the user engaged.

When needed, the app includes explicit instruction for more complex concepts that benefit from added structure. Most importantly, Duolingo remembers that people forget. Progress is fluid, meaning you can backslide if you don't participate often enough. Based on your engagement level, the app pushes refresher sessions to verify your knowledge before pushing forward.

Throw in engaging mobile notifications to remind you about the importance of continuous learning, and you have an excellent example of how reinforcement can help people learn and retain knowledge in even the most challenging subjects.

Benefits of Reinforcement

Reinforcement is more than a good idea. It's a science-backed way to improve the value and impact of any learning solution by making sure people retain and are ready to apply critical information in the moment of need. In fact, the reinforcement layer can help L&D overcome several familiar challenges.

Stop Firehosing People

I refuse to believe anyone within your organization—L&D professional or otherwise—thinks firehosing a person with hours and hours of training content is a good idea. Unfortunately, it's often the only option available. A new retail worker is brought in to fill an immediate vacancy, and they need to get on the floor ASAP. Management can only give L&D two days to complete training. But stakeholders absolutely need the new associate to know everything in the standard operating procedures. Oh, and we need to cover compliance. As a result, the employee gets blasted with 16 hours of nonstop e-learning. No one likes it, but it still must happen.

The first three layers of the MLE Framework are designed to reduce the flow of water from the proverbial information hose. L&D can still cover all the information required by stakeholders, but they don't have to cover it all at the same time or using the same method. The nice-to-know stuff is taken care of with shared knowledge and performance support. The remaining need-to-know information—now a much smaller list—is addressed using the remaining layers, including reinforcement. There's usually still too much to cover in the time available. However, reinforcement will help employees remember the most critical information after formal training is complete and they're on the job making real-life decisions.

Fit Targeted Learning Into the Flow of Work

Practice activities, such as reflection, simulation, and question-based learning, are easier to fit into the workflow compared to traditional tactics, including instructor-led sessions, online courses, and job training. These activities often require less time because they're focused on specific knowledge and skills. In addition, they must be built to align with the everyday working reality of the audience so people can fit them into their busy schedules. As a result, reinforcement—along with shared knowledge and performance support—is an impactful way to make learning an embedded part of the work experience.

Nudge People in the Right Directions

The reinforcement and coaching layers within the MLE Framework share a common attribute. They both create ongoing opportunities to nudge people toward improved performance over time. *Nudge theory* was popularized in 2008 by the Richard Thaler and Cass Sunstein book *Nudge: Improving Decisions About Health, Wealth, and Happiness*. Ongoing practice and resulting feedback are intended to influence decision making and nudge employees toward specific job behaviors. Nudge theory is sometimes attached to social engineering and the loss of free will as Daniel Kahneman warned in *Thinking Fast and Slow*. When workplace learning is focused on helping people apply behaviors that are beneficial to both themselves and the organization, this point of concern is largely moot.

Adapt Learning to Individual Needs

Duolingo is a great example of the power of reinforcement thanks to its ability to personalize learning. Because people keep coming back to the platform, Duolingo can identify areas of strength and opportunity as knowledge changes over time. The app applies machine learning to adapt training for each user so they're focused on the right topic and difficulty level at the right time. This is next-to-impossible with traditional online training because the one-and-done experience doesn't generate enough data to personalize ongoing learning.

Improve Learning Measurement

Speaking of data, reinforcement can radically improve L&D measurement. An exam may give you a snapshot of what people know immediately after training, but it doesn't show you what they know today. Ongoing reinforcement gives L&D the opportunity to measure changes in people's knowledge, skill, and behavior over time. This data, along with inputs from other sources, can be used to personalize future training, attribute the impact of learning on performance, and provide insights L&D can use to proactively adjust strategies.

Increase the Value of All Workplace Learning Activities

Reinforcement tactics can be applied on their own or as part of a structured training program. For example, you can use scenario-based questions to help retail associates learn how to respond to challenging customer situations. Or you can use a virtual reality simulation after introductory training to provide technicians with guided practice on how to use an x-ray machine. In the second example, reinforcement strengthens the value of the original training by making sure technicians retain and apply their knowledge. In the first example, reinforcement reduces the need for formal training, allowing L&D and stakeholders to focus their limited capacity on other topics that require additional resources.

Reinforcement Considerations

OK, reinforcement is a good idea with lots of benefits. So why is it potentially the most underutilized practice in workplace learning? Great question! Let's explore the most common barriers that get in the way.

Is It OK to Fail?

I ran into an unexpected challenge when I first introduced reinforcement within my learning strategy. My team used multiple-choice questions to reinforce product and process knowledge within the contact center. It was a great idea on paper, but we failed to account for employee perception. In the past, employees had only been asked to answer these kinds of questions during assessments. Those assessments had passing scores and consequences. We had inadvertently trained people to mistrust multiple-choice questions. A good practice experience includes the opportunity to fail safely for the purposes of learning. People must be free to make mistakes and improve iteratively over time. Before you introduce reinforcement tactics, reflect on your organization's perception of failure, especially as it's related to learning and development activities.

Do People Understand the Value of Practice?

Every other layer of the MLE Framework tends to feel familiar to the people with whom we work—inside and outside L&D. Reinforcement does not. In fact, it's in direct opposition to the antiquated perspective that learning is a place-and-time event. People may push back if they're asked to complete additional activities after already having been through the required training. This is why it's so important to establish a modern learning mindset before applying the full MLE Framework. People must recognize the value of learning as part of their everyday work before you ask them to make time for extra practice.

Is Time Available for Reinforcement?

Even if people buy into the value of reinforcement, L&D must still design activities that fit into the time they have available in their hectic schedules. This requires an understanding of the audience personas (there's that word again), including where people do their work, which technologies they use, and when natural downtimes occur. If a grocery employee only has five minutes available during their shift, practice activities must only require five minutes to complete. A 30-minute role-play scenario may be a value-add activity, but it won't do anyone any good if people can't find the time to use it.

Does Practice Mirror the Work Context?

Poorly designed reinforcement turns into yet another information dump. If you push employees to the same 30-minute course over and over again, they may remember a bit more over time, but they're unlikely to value the experience or retain the right information. According to Patti Shank (2017), the right type of practice must include:

- A specific goal
- Challenge that matches a person's current knowledge and skill level
- Adequate opportunity to meet the goal
- Specific feedback that focuses on development, not praise or reward

Most importantly, practice must occur in context. People must practice applying their knowledge and skills in the ways they will apply them on the job. You may develop a decent jump shot by practicing by yourself in your driveway. However, if you want to become a great basketball player, you must learn how to pull off that shot on a real court with a defender's hand in your face.

Can L&D Keep Reinforcement Current?

Like any learning content, reinforcement activities must be up to date. Unlike most learning content, this material will be in constant use. L&D must design reinforcement within the limits of their ability to maintain it. If a product or process is constantly changing, related practice activities must be easy to update. Revising a set of multiple-choice questions is a lot simpler than reworking a video-based simulation. This is another reason why it's important to focus reinforcement on very specific knowledge and skills. The chances that L&D will need to update an hour-long course covering a wide range of safety topics is much higher than a three-minute refresher video on how to properly put on personal protective equipment.

Overcoming Disruption With Reinforcement

"The illiterate of the 21st century will not be those who cannot read and write, but those who cannot learn, unlearn, and relearn."

This quote is from Alvin Toffler's 1970 book *Future Shock*. I picked it up from Clark Quinn's 2018 book *Millennials, Goldfish & Other Training Misconceptions.* Clark broke down the concept of "unlearning," which often pops up in association with disruption and change management. As the theory goes, people must be ready to unlearn what they know today to progress rapidly into the future of work. I get the idea, but I also think we're taking the concept too literally. Luckily, Clark agrees.

Learning is the new "killer app" in the workplace. In Deloitte's *2021 Global Human Capital Trends Report,* 72 percent of executives ranked "the ability of their people to adapt, reskill, and assume new roles" as the first or second most important consideration in their ability to navigate future disruptions. To keep up with the pace of change and prepare for new roles, people must continuously evolve their skills. However, this doesn't mean people should "unlearn" what they already know—even if that were physically possible. Instead, they should leverage their understanding of their current capabilities to identify gaps and prioritize the right development activities.

Reinforcement will play a critical role in helping people refine and build upon their existing skills. Practice promotes improved awareness of our strengths and opportunities. It's a chance to stretch and experiment without putting ourselves at risk. The purposeful nature of reinforcement learning reminds us that work never gets easier—we just get better.

Start Building Your Reinforcement Layer

What did you have for lunch last Tuesday? See! You still remember.

Here's how you can build up the reinforcement layer of your modern learning ecosystem and help employees remember more than their favorite lunch selections:

1. **Determine skill requirements.** To figure out the best way to help people retain their knowledge and skill, you must first determine what those knowledge and skill requirements are. Partner with stakeholders to nail down the organization's priorities over the next one to three years. Then, determine what kinds of skills employees will need to execute on those priorities. You need to at least determine the broad skill categories required, such as technical skills, conversation skills, or mechanical skills, as they will influence your reinforcement strategies.

2. **Outline the audience personas.** There is it again! Personas play a critical role when applying the MLE Framework. When it comes to the reinforcement layer, outline considerations such as audience availability, technology, and environment to help you determine how you can help people fit ongoing practice into their workflows.

3. **Match personas and skills with reinforcement tactics.** Determine which tactics best fit your audience's context and needs. Keep in mind that multiple tactics may be helpful for the audience skills and personas. For example, a mechanic may benefit from both a VR simulation of a repair process as well as multiple-choice questions that challenge them to make decisions within that process. Tactics may be used with different frequencies based on people's access, availability, and development needs.

4. **Select delivery tools.** Now that you've determined which tactics are needed to bring your reinforcement layer to life, it's time to implement the delivery tools. This may include dedicated technology, such as VR headsets, learning platforms, and simulators. Depending on your resources, you may opt to apply low-tech options, such as scenario scripts, reflection questions, and email newsletters.

5. **Build reinforcement materials.** Next up, content. Develop the materials needed to execute your selected reinforcement tactics. Remember as you build to keep in mind both the audience context (how, when, and where the content will be used) as well as ongoing content management to make sure people have continuous access to these activities.

6. **Socialize the value of practice.** You're ready to implement your reinforcement layer—almost. First, you must gain stakeholder buy-in. This includes management, subject matter experts, and employees. We'll take a closer look at influencing practices later. In the meantime, make sure people understand the value of reinforcement and how it will help them achieve their goals (as well as company KPIs) before you ask them to use their limited free time to do more training.

7. **Run experiments.** Reinforcement is usually a new L&D tactic. While you may have a grand strategy in mind, it's a good idea to start small and build the internal business case through

experimentation. Start with an audience that's usually willing to try new things and a desired result that can be easily measured. Measure the short-term impact of reinforcement over several weeks or months, including employee engagement, sentiment, knowledge growth, behavior change, and business outcomes. Use these insights to adjust your strategy on the fly and sell the concept of reinforcement to additional stakeholders.

Last Point

The longer you spend in L&D, the more you'll realize performance isn't about what you know. It's about having the confidence in your knowledge to make the right decision and transform capability into behavior. Reinforcement is an essential tactic within the modern learning ecosystem for just this reason. It supports long-term knowledge retention, builds good habits, and boosts employee confidence so that, when the moment of need arrives, people are ready to do the right thing because they've done it so many times before during practice.

In a perfect world, L&D would deliver every learning program at the exact moment of need for every employee. The content would be so well designed and people would be so highly engaged that they would remember everything and immediately apply it on the job. We don't live or work in that world. L&D must be creative in how we fit learning and support opportunities into constantly changing workflows. We must align these activities with evidence-based learning principles. And we must articulate the value of these activities so the people we support understand why continuous learning is better than firehosing people with three-hour training sessions once per quarter.

We only scratched the surface of learning science in this chapter. I hope the principles and tactics we covered provide you with enough inspiration to kickstart your own reinforcement strategy. Learning is a personal experience for each individual, and L&D must find right-fit ways to support large, diverse groups with finite resources. A lot of it comes down to the reality that the correct answer is "it depends."

How many repetitions are required in a reinforcement strategy? It depends. How far apart should reinforcement activities be spaced? It depends. Which reinforcement tactics will work best for my organization? It depends.

That's science for you!

Chapter 7

Layer 4: Coaching
Empower Managers to Guide Their Teams

SPOILER ALERT

We're going to talk about the most important people in workplace learning: managers. Specifically, we'll explore the role of coaching within the modern learning ecosystem and tackle topics such as:

- Why managers fail to support continuous learning
- The benefits of great coaching within a learning ecosystem
- Why L&D needs to build coaches, not teachers
- How to enable great coaches
- The steps to implementing your coaching layer of the MLE Framework

Coaching has been a persistent topic in my professional life.

I've designed training on coaching. I've attended sessions about coaching. I've been coached (but not as much as I should have been) and have done plenty of coaching (again, probably not as much as I should have done). However, my perspective on the value of coaching within a modern learning ecosystem didn't come from the workplace. While I discovered the importance of practices like shared knowledge, performance support, and reinforcement on the job, coaching was something I figured out in my living room.

I've struggled with my weight for most of my life. I was bullied for being the "fat kid" in grade school. It didn't matter that I had straight As or was on the varsity soccer team. My weight was all people focused on. In high school, I started playing ice hockey and lost a ton of weight. While the bullying faded away, the stigma never did.

I was super active during college and the first half of my career, always on the go with little time to relax . . . or eat. Things changed when I transitioned into L&D. I spent most of my time in meetings, in classrooms, or at my desk instead of running around movie theaters and theme parks. I was always too tired to exercise. I gained a bunch of weight. I was getting more and more uncomfortable with my health, but I couldn't figure out how to make fitness part of my regular routine. Then, I met the coach that would change my life—at 3 a.m. on cable television.

You know those ads that run late at night for workout programs, windshield repair kits, and rags that can soak up an inordinate amount of liquid? I found myself watching the same ad every night after work. It was for a workout program called Insanity, and it featured a fitness instructor named Shaun T. He was magnetic. I knew he wasn't talking to me, but it felt like he was talking to me. He totally did his job and motivated me to buy the DVD set (yes, this was pre-streaming). But it was well worth it as Shaun T. helped me turn my health around over the next few months.

I got way into Insanity. And I mean *way* into it. I was soon doing multiple HIIT (high intensity interval training) sessions every day. I reorganized my living room so I had space to burpee without smacking into the coffee table. I would do a 40-minute workout in the morning, drive to the office, do push-ups behind my desk between meetings, drive home, and then do another 25-minute session before dinner. I was all in thanks to Shaun T.

Shaun T. wasn't my personal coach. He was a person on TV leading a series of workouts recorded years prior. But he always seemed to know when I would struggle and needed encouragement to keep going. He knew how my form would falter and what I could do to improve. He knew exactly what to say and when to say it. And it always felt like he was speaking directly to me.

My daily sessions with Shaun T. helped me get my fitness back on track. I had more energy and focus throughout the day. I lost weight and felt all around better about myself. To this day, I credit Shaun T. with helping me turn things around during a very challenging period in my life.

Isn't that what a great coach is supposed to do?

—

Managers are the most important people in workplace learning and performance:

- Sure, executive buy-in is critical for scaling a modern learning strategy. But managers are more important.
- Of course, L&D must have the knowledge and skill to execute a modern learning strategy. But managers are still more important.
- Without a doubt, employees must take ownership of their own development and drive their own performance. But managers . . . you get the point.

Managers influence every part of the employee experience. They control schedules, priorities, goals, and resources. They're responsible for cascading information and keeping their teams up to date during periods of change. They're looked to for guidance and support when things get tough. They decide who's a top performer and therefore should have access to career development opportunities.

Managers are the most important people in workplace learning and performance. That's why they get their own layer in the MLE Framework: coaching (Figure 7-1).

Figure 7-1. The Coaching Layer of the MLE Framework

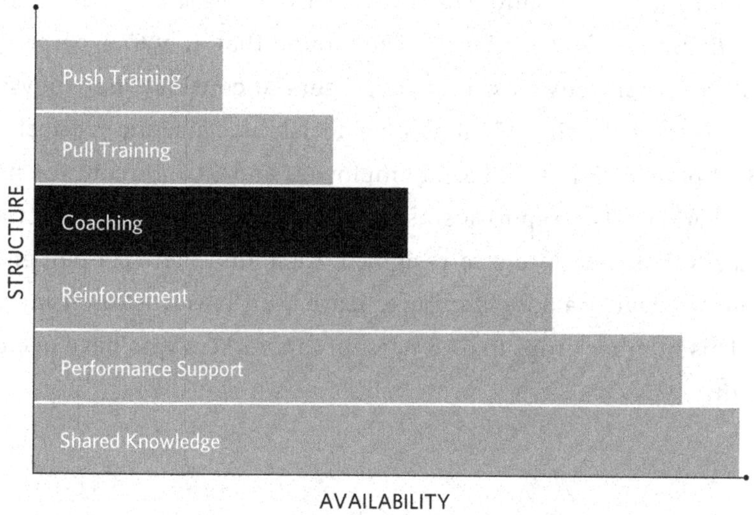

The Memeification of Management

"People don't leave jobs. They leave managers."

Have you heard this one lately? I see it shared as a meme almost daily on LinkedIn. However, this statement is a gross oversimplification of how employees make decisions. Consider your personal experience. Have you ever left a job because it was just time to try something new? Maybe you were offered an opportunity you couldn't turn down? Or perhaps you couldn't handle the travel requirements because you had to take care of a sick family member? People leave jobs for a myriad of personal and professional reasons, regardless of their relationships with their managers.

That said, people also leave because of poor management. According to Gallup's *2015 State of the American Manager* report, one in two employees have quit a job to get away from a manager at some point in their career. My experience in frontline management showed me just how much of an impact managers have on the everyday work experience. A good manager can make a mediocre job more bearable. A bad manager can make a good job untenable.

Axonify and Arlington Research surveyed frontline employees to better understand their workplace experiences, including the importance of manager relationships, as part of *The State of the Frontline Work Experience in 2021 Report*. They found that only 67.1 percent of frontline employees trust their managers to consider their physical and mental well-being when making decisions. This number declined to 59.7 percent for store-based employees and 54.2 percent for part-time workers. The report also showed a strong correlation between manager trust and intent to resign. It was found that 78.4 percent of employees who are not planning to leave their jobs trust their managers. This number drops to 57.3 percent for workers who have decided to quit.

Why Managers Fail

Another popular social media trend in talent development is the Manager vs. Leader infographic. It always includes a similar list of antithetical statements like those in Table 7-1.

Table 7-1. Tropes of "Managers vs. Leaders"

Manager	Leader
Believes in status quo	Believes in experimentation
Focuses on efficiency	Focuses on empowerment
Depends on authority	Leads with influence
Places blame	Gives credit
Develops processes	Develops people
Improves weaknesses	Focuses on strengths
Refuses to believe a hot dog is a sandwich	Open to reconsidering the nature of hot dogs

This is another oversimplification. At some point, *manager* became a bad word. Organizations want leaders instead of managers in the same way L&D wants to focus on learning instead of training. We could spend the next five pages talking about the semantics of the word *leader* and how it's a title that's earned, not assigned. Instead, let's agree that organizations need great managers to overcome disruption. After all, just because you're a manager doesn't mean that you automatically hold to the status quo or deflect blame onto others. That's what bad managers do. Improving efficiency, overcoming weaknesses, and developing processes are important parts of running an operation. Infographics like this are an unfair characterization that diminish the importance of core management skills.

In the end, the problem isn't terminology. It's the process by which managers are promoted, trained, and supported. Gallup's report found that only 18 percent of current managers have the talent required for their roles. It also highlighted the two most common reasons people become managers:

- "I was promoted because I was successful in a previous non-managerial role."

- "I have a lot of experience and tenure in my company or field."

Think about your company's management selection process. How often does it focus on key manager skills, such as establishing trust, motivating others, taking accountability, building relationships, or making decisions? Great salespeople become sales managers. Great retail associates become store managers. I was an efficient and reliable movie theater employee, so I quickly became a movie theater manager. The interview process may include questions related to manager skills, but candidates are often identified due to their ability to execute, not manage or lead.

Many managers are set up to fail from the beginning due to this skill mismatch. This problem is exacerbated when new managers do not receive timely and effective training to enable their role transition. In every management position I've ever had, I've always been in the role for months before receiving any formal training on how to do my new job. When I visit frontline operations and ask managers about their learning experiences, I always hear about people having to wait for the next training program to be scheduled. In this way, the infographics become a self-fulfilling prophecy. Managers are doing their best to get by without a real understanding of what it takes to manage a business or lead a team.

Ineffective management creates a gap in a company's ability to execute. Gallup found that managers account for at least 70 percent of the variance in employee engagement scores. This problem also creates an obstacle for L&D teams. Even the best-planned learning initiatives cannot overcome a disengaged manager. L&D needs managers at all levels to actively contribute to the learning ecosystem. They're the boots on the ground who work with employees every day. We need them to reinforce the same behaviors we promote through training. Otherwise, learning will not stick.

The good news is that L&D is in a great position to improve management development. The MLE Framework applies equally to manager training. Practices such as shared knowledge, performance support and reinforcement can enable L&D to shift from a programmatic approach to an always-on support system for managers. L&D can also empower managers to build trust, develop people, and improve business performance through a strategic approach to coaching.

3 Components of Great Coaching

Coaching is a collaborative process through which a coach helps a team member identify performance gaps, establish improvement goals, and determine appropriate next steps. This process is often facilitated by a manager with their direct reports. However, it may also be conducted by a peer or external coach.

Coaching is different than mentoring in that coaches usually have a direct working relationship with the person they are supporting. A mentor may come from any part of the organization and tends to be chosen by the mentee due to their past experience or existing relationship. Coaching is also not the same as teaching. *Teaching* is an educational activity focused on the acquisition of knowledge. *Coaching* is an operational activity meant to help people continuously refine their skills and achieve their goals through performance.

There are plenty of coaching models out there. Your organization may use GROW (goal, reality, options, will) or FUEL (frame, understand, explore, lay out) or STEPPPA (subject, target, emotion, perception, plan, pace, action). Regardless, an effective coaching strategy is built on three main components: insight, skill, and priority.

- **Insight.** Job feedback often lacks context and is heavily based on end results. Coaches need access to data and reporting so they can proactively identify performance gaps, determine right-fit solutions, and track progress in collaboration with their team members before business KPIs are negatively impacted.
- **Skill.** Coaches must develop the skills needed to facilitate impactful coaching interactions. This includes the ability to build trust, ask good questions, actively listen, recognize strengths, monitor emotions, demonstrate care, and communicate recommendations.
- **Priority.** Coaches need time to focus on their team members. If they're constantly distracted by operational demands, their employee relationships will suffer. Humu's *State of the Manager 2022 Report* found a disconnect between organizational and management priorities. Managers often struggle with the

fundamentals, such as hiring, retention, and burnout, while the company pushes broader themes like agility and transformation. Organizations must prioritize coaching as an essential part of the job and afford the time needed for skill development, preparation, and engagement.

The best way to get people to think differently about workplace learning is to help them do their jobs better and achieve their goals. When it comes to managers, L&D can build champions by helping them become better coaches capable of improving team performance. This means rethinking how we approach management development and enablement based on the core coaching components:

- **Insight**
  - Partner with data experts to provide managers with improved reporting on employee performance, including dashboards that highlight the leading indicators of business outcomes.
  - Improve learning measurement to provide a more holistic perspective on performance, including insights into employee engagement, knowledge growth, and on-the-job performance.
  - Use reporting technology to provide managers with actionable insights and recommendations for areas of coaching focus.
- **Skill**
  - Offer development opportunities on related topics, including coaching skills, before people step into management roles.
  - Provide managers with practice opportunities to improve their coaching skills.
- **Priority**
  - Shift from a programmatic approach to management training to a continuous learning system that offers managers ongoing support, including shared knowledge, performance support, and reinforcement.
  - Introduce coaching technology to augment human conversations with always-on digital support.

The specific tools and tactics you should apply will vary based on your organizational context. In any case, L&D must focus on these three key components—insights, skill, priority—to activate the coaching layer of the modern learning ecosystem.

Coaching in Real Life: Peloton

Yes, this is another coaching example from the fitness world. What can I say? L&D should borrow more practices from athletics when it comes to coaching.

Years after my Shaun T. experience, I was once again part of an exceptional coaching relationship. This time, I found my coach on a stationary bicycle.

I had never ridden a bike before—of any kind. I'm not kidding. Apparently, I never had a childhood because I never attempted to ride a bike.

The first time I sat on a bicycle seat was when my household acquired a Peloton during the pandemic. We all worked from home and struggled with the sedentary lifestyle. We decided to check out the latest and greatest in-home workout technology and bought into the Peloton trend.

Peloton quickly became my new personal fitness coach:

- The app recommended workouts based on my history, preferences, and available time.
- The instructors provided guidance to improve my form, maximize my effort, and motivate me to finish the workout.
- The bike tracked my progress during the ride and tracked my progress over time.

Peloton applies the three components of effective coaching to sustain my fitness habit and guide me toward improved results. And they're taking it up a notch with their Guide device. This set-top camera tracks your movements as you complete workouts. It then provides feedback on your performance—just like a personal coach. It can't do everything a human trainer can do, but it provides a level of personalized coaching that was previously impossible at the scale necessary to support people who prefer to exercise at home.

L&D should take inspiration from fitness technology to provide meaningful, personalized coaching at the speed and scale of the modern workplace.

Benefits of Coaching

That was a quick breakdown of what it takes to empower coaches within the learning ecosystem. Here's why the coaching layer of the MLE Framework must be a top priority if L&D hopes to foster a disruption-ready workplace.

Build Trust and Accountability

Few things about the workplace are more frustrating than a manager who refuses to hold people accountable for their performance. This dereliction of duty erodes employee trust in the organization and inhibits the potential impact of L&D initiatives. Managers are expected to coach their teams, but they must have the knowledge and confidence to do so. L&D support is essential, especially for new and inexperienced managers.

Add Local Context to Learning

Data and technology enable L&D to deliver learning experiences that are more personalized than ever before. Adaptive learning allows us to provide the right resource to the right person at the right time. However, even the best technology has its limits. L&D is often several steps removed from the operation. We don't know what's happening in the store, on the manufacturing line, or in the home office on any given day. Managers do. They can take context into account during their coaching interactions to provide the best possible version of personalized support.

Nudge People in the Right Direction

The MLE Framework is designed to cut off the training firehose and provide just the right amount of information to help people solve problems and develop their skills. It helps people learn and grow over time, because that's how the brain works. Coaching is an essential part of this strategy. Targeted feedback provided in the workflow can nudge people to iteratively improve their performance. Rather than hitting someone with everything they did wrong during an annual performance review, coaching focuses on their most important opportunities in the moment to guide (not shove) them back onto the path to achieving their goals.

Uncover New Employee Needs

An effective L&D team uses a variety of inputs to shape their learning strategies and priorities. This includes stakeholder requests, operational data, marketplace research, and employee feedback. Manager insights are another important input L&D must include in their decision making. Managers have hands-on knowledge of the factors that most influence employee performance. They know what works and what doesn't in real life. L&D must continuously engage managers to uncover hidden performance gaps and design solutions that align with manager expectations.

Support Ongoing Manager Buy-In

Why should managers support L&D initiatives if they don't get any personal value from them? It's the classic "what have you done for me lately" scenario. L&D may prepare manager versions of programs, provide talking points and FAQs, and distribute reports on who has not completed the training by the due date. This doesn't count as including managers in your learning strategy. This makes L&D look like just another task on another already overloaded list. L&D must prioritize managers within their ecosystem by providing support on critical job functions, including coaching. Show managers how you can help them achieve their goals, and they'll support projects designed to improve their team's performance. Fair deal.

Coaching Considerations

Coaching has always been in my top five for most-requested training topics. Every company seems to prioritize coaching, but they never seem to improve coaching behaviors because they keep asking for more training. To make coaching an integral part of continuous learning, L&D must answer some important questions.

How Are Managers Held Accountable for Employee Development?

There's a popular quote attributed to Peter Drucker that goes, "What gets measured gets managed." Well, Drucker never said that, and it's a flawed idea. However, there's a much less popular quote from JD Dillon that goes, "Whatever measurements are used to determine someone's compensation or job status will get a lot more attention than everything else." If managers are measured solely based on business KPIs like sales revenue and net promoter scores, they will find the most direct routes to achieving those goals. It's just the way people work.

If we want managers to prioritize future-focused ideas like employee development and coaching, we must find ways to hold them accountable. Improved measurement practices, such as data that indicates employee skill progression, engagement, and company bench strength, can be used alongside traditional KPIs to reflect a manager's total contribution to the business. If they're compensated based on how effectively they support their team, managers will be more likely to put in the necessary effort.

Are Managers Provided With the Time Needed to Coach Effectively?

Managers are always busy doing "manager stuff." They have meetings to attend. They have interviews to conduct. They have to call the supplier because the last order was messed up. And the guy in aisle four wants to speak with a manager right away. Managers have a lot going on. Unfortunately, the people side of their roles often gets sidelined by the operational stuff. If we want them to dedicate more effort toward coaching, we need to make sure they have the time to do it.

Before you ask managers to take on an additional task (even if it's a super important one that's supposed to be part of their jobs already), find out if they'll actually be able to do it. Talk to them about their workflow and how you may be able to help free up the capacity they need to focus on coaching. Partner with operations stakeholders to make sure management tasks are properly prioritized and employees are moved to the top of the list (but not before they deal with the guy in aisle four).

Do Managers Have Opportunities to Practice Coaching?

Coaching is part of most management training programs. That means every manager must be great at it, right? Managers may learn how to execute a coaching model in the classroom, but how often do they get a chance to practice and make mistakes before they interact with employees? Make sure managers have access to the reinforcement layer within the MLE Framework to improve their coaching behaviors. Give them quick and easy ways to practice, such as the option to schedule voluntary role-play sessions or a series of online practice scenarios. It's up to the manager to make sure they have the skills needed to be an effective coach, but L&D can provide low-risk opportunities to refine these skills as they're developed on the job.

Do Managers Have the Data Needed to Coach Effectively?

The amount of data managers use on the job to coach their teams often varies by function. A contact center manager may have a lot of performance-related data while a warehouse manager only has stats related to safety incidents and on-time shipments. A great coach takes a performer's entire experience into account, not just their end results. Make sure any relevant performance data that could be used to inform coaching conversations, such as behavior observations and skills development, is as easily accessible to managers as standard business KPIs. Help managers take a 360-degree perspective on performance, even if they're not always there to witness it themselves.

Overcoming Disruption With Coaching

"They're broken."

This is how a retail executive responded when I asked how their store managers were feeling almost two years into the COVID-19 pandemic. The frontline workforce had spent that time dealing with nonstop safety concerns and business changes. Now, they were dealing with staffing shortages as they did everything they could to keep the doors open. Their managers stood alongside them the entire time, doing their best to take care of their teams in the midst of unprecedented disruption.

The manager is the face of the company for many employees, especially those who are far removed from the corporate office. "If you have any questions, speak with your manager" is one of the most common phrases used during change management initiatives. Most managers don't make the big decisions for the company, but they play a pivotal role in bringing those decisions to life. That includes guiding the performance of their teams as the workplace continues to change around them.

If we want employees to do their best work, we need to make sure they feel taken care of. Support services like HR have a role to play, but it's ultimately up to the manager to demonstrate empathy, compassion, and competence as the personification of the company. That's why it's critical for organizations to not take their managers for granted and instead make sure they have the support needed to help them be there for their people.

L&D needs managers to act as champions within the modern learning ecosystem. But first, we must show managers that we're here to help them by providing the training and tools they need to feel taken care of too.

Start Building Your Coaching Layer

Now that we've covered the benefits of coaching and some practical considerations, let's run through how you can add the coaching layer to your learning ecosystem.

1. **Assess your coaching culture.** Partner with stakeholders to determine the current status of your organization's coaching culture. Ask employees how often they receive actionable feedback about their performance. Ask managers how prepared they feel to engage team members in coaching conversations. Use your findings as a baseline for building the coaching system.

2. **Establish coaching expectations.** Determine the role coaching should play within your organization. Work with stakeholders to identify right-fit coaching practices for the audiences you support, including any preferred models or processes. Partner

with HR to determine the connection between ongoing coaching and performance management.

3. **Identify insight needs and data sources.** Determine how data can be used to inform your selection of coaching practices. Assess your learning and operational data practices to choose the right measures related to employee performance. Partner with data experts, such as business operations or external providers, to build actionable reporting dashboards for managers to use while planning and facilitating coaching conversations.

4. **Provide skill development and practice opportunities.** Integrate coaching into your management learning programs. Apply the MLE Framework to create a blended experience with on-demand (shared knowledge, performance support) and programmatic (reinforcement, push and pull training) elements as needed. Include practice opportunities, such as interactive scenarios and role plays, that new and experienced managers can use to refine their coaching skills.

5. **Introduce support tools and technology.** RedThread Research's 2021 report *Coaching Tech: The Human and the Robots* points to a combination of resources and philosophy as the driving factors in selecting right-fit coaching tools. If your organization lacks the capacity to provide the desired level of coaching support, consider "coaching-as-a-service" options like chatbots or external providers to close the gap. However, if managers have the time and capacity to provide individual coaching, your selected tools should augment these one-on-one engagements through features such as meeting planning, goal setting, and progress tracking.

6. **Measure coaching effectiveness.** Just because coaching is happening doesn't mean it's yielding the desired results. Collect qualitative and quantitative data to measure coaching effectiveness. Conduct surveys to find out how employees and managers feel about their coaching experiences. Use

learning data to track manager improvements during training and practice activities. Correlate coaching engagement with changes in job behavior and performance outcomes to determine potential business impact.

Last Point

Did I mention that managers are the most important people in workplace learning and performance?

Hopefully you recognize the importance of their role as coaches within the modern learning ecosystem. L&D can amplify our impact by helping managers improve in this essential part of their roles. By proxy, we can provide every employee with personalized support beyond the capabilities of even the best learning technology.

Chapter 8

Layers 5 and 6: Pull and Push Training

Make Structured Training the Last Resort

We've finally reached the part of the MLE Framework where L&D spends most of its time—formal training. Instead of talking about how to build better courses, let's explore a few strategic ways L&D can improve our structured training solutions, including:

- When to push or pull structured training
- How microlearning principles apply to all learning solutions
- How to improve compliance training while still checking the box
- How the 3B approach can help you deploy training faster
- How to strengthen the push and pull training layers within your learning ecosystem

Did you know I was once the highest rated L&D facilitator at the Walt Disney World Resort? It's true! I rocked a consistent 4.9 out of 5 in my Level 1 surveys. It's a totally meaningless humblebrag, but the fact that I remember it explains my professional mindset in 2008.

Back then, my L&D team had just executed the largest training initiative in the history of the resort. We delivered two-hour instructor-led sessions to every operations cast member and manager on property as part of the company's wholesale revamp of guest service standards. That's more than 40,000 classroom participants in less than a year.

Feedback was great. Executives loved the program. We were in full celebration mode once implementation wrapped up. The company even hosted a recognition dinner for L&D at Epcot complete with a dessert party and private fireworks viewing. I have a picture from that night with me, an executive, and Mickey Mouse holding the statue that now sits prominently in the background of my home office. We were at the top of the proverbial L&D mountain. But what do they say about everything that goes up?

The size of our project team was reduced shortly thereafter. Most of our facilitators returned to their operational roles. We maintained enough capacity to deliver sessions to newly hired cast members. The team went into autopilot, delivering the same sessions over and over again. I still loved the work we were doing, inspiring cast members to deliver exceptional experiences for guests from all over the world. Nevertheless, I felt like we were stuck in place. After all, one class couldn't change results long-term, could it?

This was the first time in my career that I was unable to personally observe the end results of training. As an operations manager and HR partner, I had always played an active part in fostering and sustaining behavior change. I designed the training, delivered the training, coached employees after the training, and measured business results related to the training. This time, I was part of a central L&D team delivering courses for people in every line of business—from retail and food service to attractions and housekeeping. Once people left my classroom, I typically never saw them again. I had no way of knowing if they applied what they learned, or if they retained anything at all from our time together. If I was experiencing this level of uncertainty, surely the rest of the L&D team had considered it.

I went to my boss and asked the question that had been on my mind since that night at Epcot: What happens next? The answer: Nothing. Our mandate was to keep doing what we were doing. People liked the classes (4.9 out of 5.0, after all), so we were going to keep delivering them until further notice. That answer didn't sit well with me. There had to be more we could do to make sure the things we taught stuck long-term. Many of my team members agreed with my perspective, but we couldn't shift the direction of the project given how popular it was across the company.

So I started looking for ways to build upon our success and sustain the impact of our training.

That's when I met Kim Possible.

Disney was planning a new *Kim Possible*–themed attraction at Epcot, and the management team wanted to include guest service training as part of their onboarding program. They turned to my L&D group due to the popularity of our classes on the subject. My boss knew I wanted to take on more instructional design work, so he assigned me the task of creating a custom program for the cast of the Kim Possible World Showcase Adventure. This project would end up shaping my perspective on structured training for the rest of my career.

Management wanted a two-hour instructor-led session. That was what they'd seen us do before. That was what they knew. That was what I was expected to deliver. I didn't argue. Plus, at that point in my career, I only really knew how to design and deliver instructor-led training (ILT) and on-the-job training (OJT). I didn't have access to e-learning developers, mobile devices, or other tools needed to pull off a blended experience. So I built the most interactive classroom session anyone at the resort had ever seen (at least in my opinion). The PowerPoint was a mix of highly themed graphics and videos. I challenged participants to apply their guest service skills to defeat a made-up super villain who was terrorizing guests at Epcot in a very PG way (stealing strollers, littering, and so on). We even went on-location for part of the session, practicing our skills in the real job environment. It's still the best course I've ever created. But it wasn't the classroom materials that made it so important to my professional development. It was the way I approached the design that made a real difference moving forward.

I knew the ILT would be a big deal during the opening process for the attraction. Then, it would more than likely get eliminated after a few months to reduce costs. That meant cast members who joined the team after opening wouldn't get the same training experience. It would be up to the location trainers and managers to foster the right job behaviors, and we all know how inconsistent that can become over time. That's why I built sustainment tactics into the program from the start. I designed a themed poster with key takeaways from the session to post in the attraction's break areas. I created a translation cheat sheet with themed language for the attraction to emphasize storytelling. For example, a guest ticket became a "passport" because scanning it at the attraction kickstarted their world showcase adventure. Finally, I provided a pocket-sized coaching guide managers could use to observe and reinforce desired job behaviors during everyday conversations.

By all accounts, the classroom session was great. It jumpstarted people's experience at a new attraction and introduced a range of new guest service tactics. But it was still just two hours in a room with an instructor who wasn't part of the team. The additional support materials gave cast members the best possible chance to retain and apply what they learned on the job. Yes, it was up to management to use the tools. Still, I walked away from Kim Possible feeling like I had provided a workplace learning experience that could be sustained long-term without L&D. I also realized how critical it is to align new tactics (performance support tools) with concepts stakeholders already understand and appreciate (ILT, OJT) when you're trying to get people to think differently about the way learning happens at work.

And now you won't be able to get the *Kim Possible* theme song out of your head for the rest of the day.

———

I have a confession. This was the most difficult chapter for me to write in the entire book.

It's not because it's chock-full of awesome information. It's because I don't have much to say about structured training. I've been writing about, presenting, and applying the MLE Framework for half of my career. When I get to these top two layers during a session, I typically say something like "And here's where the standard L&D stuff fits" before quickly moving on (Figure 8-1).

I've never gone more in-depth about what's included in these layers because this is where L&D spends most of our time. Push and pull training include a list of familiar tactics, such as:

- Job training

- Classroom sessions
- E-learning
- Webinars
- Off-the-shelf courses
- Job shadowing
- Development programs
- Apprenticeships

Figure 8-1. Push and Pull Training: The Most Familiar Layers of the MLE Framework

In this chapter, I'm not going to tell you how to design a good virtual ILT or build an effective online course. There are plenty of other smart people who cover that stuff. This book—and the entire MLE Framework— is designed to help you reduce your reliance on structured training. At this point, you've hopefully realized the limitations of these layers and are looking for ways to spend less time and resources on them.

That said, just because we apply these tactics all the time doesn't mean we're hitting the mark. The MLE Framework doesn't eliminate the need for great structured training. It simply reduces the need for it when addressing performance challenges. Even then, structured training should never function in isolation. Rather, it must be designed in alignment with the other layers of the framework. We'll cover more about MLE application in the next two chapters. For now, let's explore principles that can help L&D improve structured training when it's the right-fit or required solution (Figure 8-1).

Push vs. Pull

Required completion. That's the difference between push and pull training. These two layers apply the same tactics and content types. For example, both layers may include online courses, instructor-led sessions, and hands-on training programs. The only difference is that, in the push layer, people are required to complete the training while, in the pull layer, people have the option to do it. Push training is added to an employee's path with a deadline while pull training sits on the shelf, waiting to be accessed.

The push vs. pull dynamic is present throughout the MLE Framework. Shared knowledge and performance support primarily focus on pull tactics that people can leverage in the moment of need. Reinforcement and coaching lean more toward push activities that are directed at employees to support specific outcomes. The push and pull layers are unique because they include structured training activities with clear objectives and set beginnings and ends. An employee can pull a job aid on demand and use it as needed to support their everyday work. To complete a course, they must progress through a series of predetermined steps over a set period. Even if a course is adaptive or self-paced, the employee still has limited control over how it can be used. An instructional designer has already made most of these decisions for them.

Push training is often associated with compliance, which we'll talk about in a few pages. Pull training is commonly related to self-directed learning and career development. Employees need both and more to be successful over the short and long-term. They need access to the right learning and support opportunities at the right time. Sometimes, that moment is dictated to them, as is the case with new employee onboarding. Other times, they get to make the call, such as when they decide to pursue additional skill development to support a change in career direction.

So, how much should you use the push and pull layers? Should you target a specific percentage for each? Is one inherently better than the other? This is yet another case of "it depends." Some L&D pros contend that workplace learning should be a primarily pull experience driven by personal curiosity, ongoing discovery, and implicit motivation. I don't disagree with them—which is a cagey way of saying I don't entirely agree either. There's no set formula for how much of what kind of training an employee needs. Some people require structure and guidance to build specific skills while they leverage on-demand resources to develop others.

The MLE Framework includes a blend of push and pull tactics to help you balance your own ecosystem. Even when a learning experience must be structured in a particular way (for example, a highly regulated compliance course), it can usually be supported and sustained using less structured tactics (such as job aids, performance support, and coaching). Every learning ecosystem should contain push and pull learning opportunities, but how and when structured training is required is highly dependent on the problem you're trying to solve and the context associated with it.

Let's Talk About Microlearning

All structured training should be microlearning. You probably reacted to that statement in one of three ways:

1. You nodded your head vigorously because you're a microlearning stan.
2. You verbally scoffed at my assertion because you don't think microlearning is a real thing.
3. You took a photo of the sentence to share on social media because you think I need to be called out for being a shill for BIG MICROLEARNING.

Let's get something out of the way: Under no circumstances should all workplace training be less than 10 minutes in duration. You can't learn how to execute complex tasks in less than 10 minutes. Thankfully, microlearning isn't about duration, despite what you may have been led to believe.

Yes, there are many, many courses out there that are way, way too long. The MLE Framework is designed to help you fit learning and support into the everyday workflow, but that doesn't mean all content must be artificially brief. Rather, all learning content and experiences—including push and pull training—should be designed based on six microlearning principles: focus, familiarity, science, access, format, and data. (Figure 8-2).

Figure 8-2. The Six Microlearning Principles

| Focus | Familiarity | Science | Access | Format | Data |

1. Focus

All content must be designed to solve a specific problem. There must be a clear, defined, agreed-upon goal before a solution can be selected. The narrower the better. For example, rather than build a course called "Safety in the Workplace" that covers a wide range of concepts within a single module, instructional designers should break the concept down into specific topics. This may include topics like personal protective equipment, cleaning up spills, and ladder safety. You may be able to address each topic with the same type of content, or different topics may benefit from different solutions. Plus, when training is modularized in this way, you can stack topics together to create more substantial programs. All the boxes get checked while the learning experience is easier to fit into the limited time people have available on the job. This focus on a specific outcome is what naturally makes microlearning shorter than traditional courses.

2. Familiarity

Have you ever considered what it's like to log into an LMS you rarely use, click through a transcript of strangely titled courses, open a SCORM module that launches three additional browser tabs, and complete a tutorial on how to navigate training content designed with a UI you've never seen before? This is what workplace learning looks like for too many employees: a totally foreign experience that's nothing like the content experiences they have every day through apps like YouTube, Disney+, and TikTok. Training should be challenging to keep people engaged and help them learn, but it shouldn't be difficult to use. L&D must leverage familiarity in our learning experience design—including both content and technology. When the experience feels simple, people can focus on what they're meant to learn.

3. Science

We already covered learning science basics like spacing, repetition, and interleaving within the reinforcement layer. These principles must be the foundation of everything L&D does, including structured training. People simply cannot retain all the information delivered during a 45-minute online course, a two-hour instructor-led session, or an eight-hour job training shift. L&D must use proven learning science principles to create blended experiences that leverage every layer within the MLE Framework to ensure long-term knowledge retention and behavior change.

4. Access

It doesn't matter how well designed a course is if people can't access it. This is why personas (there it is again) are a critical part of applying the MLE Framework (if you hadn't heard). L&D must understand the everyday workplace realities of the audiences we support. This includes how and where people spend their time, how their tasks are managed, which devices they use to access information, and how they're motivated to perform. Our learning experiences must be designed to fit within these realities if we hope to drive engagement, knowledge growth, and skill application. There's a reason I've said this so many times up to this point!

5. Format

How do you select the format for a particular piece of content? L&D should make this decision based on the specific needs of their audience as well as the nature of the skills being developed. For example, a video may be a great choice for a contact center audience trying to learn how to overcome a popular customer objection because they sit at a computer and can easily watch the video as intended. However, this format may be a bad option for a manufacturing worker who needs to review a new safety procedure, because they don't regularly use devices that can play video and they work in a noisy, safety-critical environment. Stakeholders, technology, and circumstances may sometimes limit L&D's options, but we should always do our best to match the format to the message and audience.

6. Data

There's an entire chapter about data coming up, but it could easily be the subject of this entire book. Measurement is the biggest gap in L&D capability today because it's such an important part of making informed decisions. Data should help L&D design solutions that focus on specific, proven employee needs. When a stakeholder requests a course that covers an unrealistic amount of information, data can help us focus the conversation on the knowledge and behaviors that will actually help the organization achieve the desired outcome.

That's it. That's what microlearning actually is. These six principles will help you shift away from structured training that's hours, days, or weeks long to targeted solutions that better fit into the everyday work experience.

Do you need to use the word *microlearning* to apply these principles? Absolutely not! That's why microlearning was never a real thing. It's just a buzzy term that helps L&D pros shift our focus toward proven principles like these to provide right-fit solutions. But if using a made-up word helps us get rid of the fluff and provide employees with better support, let's keep talking about microlearning. But please don't try to make macrolearning a thing!

Getting Better at Compliance

There's a reason so many of the questions I get after conference sessions are prefaced by "I work in a highly regulated industry . . . "

Compliance is an unavoidable reality of our profession. Regulators exist. Companies have lawyers. Risk is part of work. Compliance training will never go away, but that doesn't mean we can't get at least a little better at how we handle it.

First, let's clarify what *compliance* means. This term often gets attached to any and all forms of required training. L&D and HR may have a specific definition in mind when they talk about compliance, but I often hear operational managers use the term to refer to every training program the company requires employees to complete. This not only muddies the concept of compliance training, but it also tells you a lot about how structured training is perceived within an organization.

Let's break compliance training into three distinct categories:

- Training required by an external regulator (*regulatory training*)
- Training required by an internal stakeholder (*mandated training*)
- Training required before a person can execute the requirements of their role (*job training*)

L&D's goal is to provide employees with the knowledge and skills required to do their jobs safely and effectively while mitigating potential risk for the company. Therefore, you must approach each category of compliance training based on its unique considerations:

- **Regulatory training** is dictated by an external stakeholder. You probably don't know them, and they probably don't know you, your company, or your training practices. Therefore, your options are limited when it comes to improving the push training experience. If the law states that employees must complete a specific online course and record two hours of seat time per year, then L&D must execute this requirement in the most seamless way possible. This is further complicated when different regions or functions operate under different regulations. California may require one course while New York requires another. L&D must partner with internal stakeholders to understand these regulations and apply the best possible solution, even if you know employees will not retain most of the information delivered during the two-hour online course.

- **Mandated training** is often added on top of regulatory requirements. The law says employees must complete one course, but your internal compliance team decided to add three extra modules to make absolutely sure the company is protected. This category provides more wiggle room for L&D to introduce improved solutions. You may not be able to remove the mandate altogether, but you could shift your internal stakeholder's mindset when it comes to how the mandate is addressed.

- **Job training** isn't really about "compliance." It still fits within the push training layer, but it's about the knowledge and skill development activities an employee is required to complete before they are ready for an essential job function. For example, if an employee must operate a baler to bundle cardboard as part of their everyday work, they must complete the necessary training to be certified to use that piece of equipment. L&D must apply modern learning practices to make sure all stakeholders understand why this training is critical so it is not perceived as a nonproductive use of time.

L&D can apply the same process across the spectrum of required workplace training to improve the employee experience while still checking all the necessary boxes and reducing the strain on their own limited resources:

1. **Clarify the requirement.** What does the rule actually say? Did an external regulator decide how this requirement must be met, or was the rule interpreted by an internal stakeholder? You can't improve the compliance experience until you understand why it exists in the first place. Talk to the people responsible for

verifying that the training is completed, such as your legal or compliance team.

2. **Connect to job performance.** How does the requirement relate to an employee's job performance? Does it connect to specific products or processes, or is it a general requirement that employees must always keep in mind at work? Clarifying this point will help you position your solution as close to the moment of performance as possible.

3. **Expand solution options.** How was the current training solution chosen? If it's mandated by an external regulator, you may not have much room for improvement. However, if it was at least partially dictated internally, you can seize the opportunity to help your stakeholders think differently about how you address the requirement. For example, when the current two-hour annual course was designed, courses may have been the only option available for the required audience. Today, you likely have more solution options available to solve the same problem that are just as—if not more—effective. However, your stakeholder (who isn't an L&D professional) probably doesn't know that.

4. **Reinforce critical knowledge and behavior.** Even if you must deliver a specific solution, it usually doesn't mean that's all you're allowed to do to address the performance challenges related to the topic. Augment your push training with the other layers of the MLE Framework so employees retain the right information and make good decisions on the job. For example, use the questions from an end-of-course assessment to build ongoing reinforcement activities. There's a reason the required training is required. Make sure you give your employees the best opportunity to meet their job requirements, not just check training boxes.

5. **Reporting meaningful results.** You must provide reporting that shows all the boxes have been checked, but that doesn't mean that's the only data you should provide regarding the

impact of your required training. For example, if you deliver ongoing reinforcement for critical compliance topics, use the resulting data to report on current knowledge levels within your workforce. Improved reporting can really help shift people's mindsets. What's more important, whether an employee completed a course six months ago or whether they know to perform their job in a way that's compliant with any laws or regulations?

6. **Automate the process whenever possible.** Even simple compliance training programs can take up a lot of L&D capacity. Look for ways to automate administration whenever possible. Automated reporting eliminates the need to extract data from the LMS and send spreadsheets to managers to track down delinquent employees. Automated delivery can also make it easier to fit compliance training into the workflow. Once learning becomes an embedded part of everyday work through the MLE Framework, compliance topics can be introduced seamlessly, without the need for separate projects and communications.

7. **Be open and honest.** This may be number seven on the list, but it's the most important tactic for improving people's experience with compliance training. Be honest. If you're required to make people attend a class that you know is boring and tedious, tell employees that you're required to do it. Explain why the training is important for them and the company without trying to make it sound more exciting or interesting than it really is. Thank employees for their time and attention, and do your best to make sure these "compliance moments" are the exception rather than the rule when it comes to their experience with L&D.

There will always be required training. Regulations will never go away. Stakeholders will always have mandates. Compliance will just get more complex with each passing year. Checking boxes and mitigating risk is a big part of what L&D does. It just shouldn't be all that we do within a modern learning ecosystem.

The 3B Content Strategy

Measurement is the biggest tactical challenge facing L&D. Compliance comes in second. Content is a close third. Some organizations employ an army of designers and developers and spend millions of dollars every year building and maintaining instructional content. Others rely heavily on pre-built, off-the-shelf (OTS) content due to the lack of development capacity within the organization. And then there are companies that have internal resources but choose to outsource some or all of their content development.

Regardless of approach, every organization is trying to answer the same question: How can I provide the right content to the right person at the right time? This is a hard problem to solve, even if you do have a pile of resources. Great content is hard to build. Knowledge and skill requirements are always changing. Stakeholders are difficult to please. This reality leads to a time-consuming, often expensive, seemingly never-ending content quandary. Many L&D teams get backed into a corner and find themselves building one-size-fits-all courses rather than personalized solutions. Is it better to provide something for everyone rather than focusing on just a few audiences if what you end up providing isn't the right thing for anyone? That's how convoluted L&D's content struggle often gets.

So, what's the best option for solving the content problem?

a) Should L&D invest in development resources and build custom solutions as fast as they can?

b) Should L&D outsource solution development to those with more resources or specialized subject matter expertise?

c) Should L&D do the "Netflix thing," aggregate content from OTS catalogs and let employees pull what they need?

The answer is D—all of the above!

Content is a complex problem that requires a complex but strategic solution. L&D must leverage the full range of options within the workplace ecosystem. You must apply a consistent process to determine when a topic should be addressed with internal content and when it can be covered with external resources. L&D must apply the 3B Curation Method (Figure 8-3).

Figure 8-3. The 3B Curation Method

Borrow   Buy   Build

Let's explore the 3B content curation method using everyone's favorite workplace learning topic: Microsoft Excel.

Borrow

Is this topic general enough to leverage open resources and crowdsourced knowledge? Borrow it.

This is what many people think of when it comes to curation: aggregating solutions from openly available sources to solve more problems faster. It's a great approach . . . sometimes. The "crowd" can usually provide information faster than L&D can build it. However, despite what people like to say, the crowd isn't always the smartest person in the room. Sometimes, a problem requires established expertise. You must consider all available crowdsourcing options before narrowing your focus to more structured offerings.

For example, a team comes to L&D asking for training in Microsoft Excel. Sure, L&D could spend time, money, and resources building custom Excel training just for them, but this is a pretty general topic. Someone must already have the content on this. Sure enough, L&D finds an internal SME on Excel who is willing to provide tutorials on specific software skills. L&D borrows their expertise by scheduling a series of virtual sessions with the SME and pre-records a session that can then be accessed on-demand.

Buy

Has a trustworthy partner already solved this problem, making it more efficient to leverage their OTS expertise? Buy it.

There are dozens of providers selling thousands of OTS courses. Classroom, virtual, e-learning—they offer it all. However, their expertise comes at a price. Therefore, L&D must be strategic to maximize their limited budget when purchasing (or licensing) OTS content. This is usually a solid option when addressing common, durable skills—topics that are consistent across businesses or industries. For example, no one should ever have to build a ladder safety training again. That problem has already been solved and is available for purchase in every possible format. Buying is also a great way to address regulatory topics that require specific solutions or change frequently. Rather than dedicating valuable L&D capacity to keeping up with regional laws, you can outsource this process to a specialized provider.

Back to our Excel example. L&D finds that the SME's session covers more nuanced Excel skills. However, some employees lack the fundamental knowledge needed to keep up with these more advanced tutorials. There's plenty of open content on YouTube, but it's inconsistent in terms of production quality. Plus, it could vanish at any time. So, L&D licenses a series of foundational Excel courses from an OTS provider. Rather than acquire an entire content library they're unlikely to use, L&D pays based on content usage with the option to add or reduce seat counts by topic as needed.

Build

Is the topic or application of knowledge and skill unique to your organization? Build it.

This is the last resort. OTS and crowdsourced content cover lots of topics, but there might be something different about this topic within your business that requires a unique solution. It could be a product only your company sells, a process your company developed, or a standard only your employees must follow. This means it's time to design and develop your own solution. You could do this with your own team or outsource custom development to a third party, depending on your available resources and the timeliness of the problem you're trying to solve. Keep in mind that the build option requires not only the development of custom content but also investment in continued maintenance that is often not required with the buy option.

Let's wrap up our Excel example. L&D borrowed internal expertise and bought OTS content. However, there's still a gap in their learning content strategy. The internal SME isn't familiar with a few nuanced processes employees are expected to complete using Excel. This also isn't covered in the OTS content because the processes are specific to this company. L&D decides to build a supplementary set of videos and job aids covering the proprietary processes. They curate the various content objects together within a learning path in the LMS but allow employees to pick and choose which items they need based on their existing Excel knowledge. L&D also makes the path available to other audiences so they can request it as on-demand training if needed. L&D will just need to consider how to pay for the additional licenses to access the OTS content within the path should more teams request the training.

Borrow, buy, or build? Some content problems can be solved with one option. However, when L&D can strategically balance all three, you're able to provide faster access to more targeted solutions without requiring extensive talent and budgetary resources. By applying a curation mindset, you can mix and match the 3Bs to get the right content to the right people at the right time.

Start Building Your Push and Pull Layers

We haven't reinvented the wheel in this chapter, but with any luck I've given you enough to think about so you're better prepared when you need to turn to the push and pull training layers in your learning ecosystem. Here's how to get started:

1. **Assess your required training.** Take a hard look at your current training offerings. What process did you use to arrive

at a structured training solution? Do you start with this option by default, or do you use a results-based approach to match a right-fit solution with the intended audience and desired outcome? This will help you decide whether structured content is truly required, or if other layers of the MLE Framework can be applied in the future to replace unnecessary push or pull training.

2. **Implement microlearning principles.** Look for ways to break lengthy courses and programs into focused, stackable modules. Yes, this will probably reduce the duration of your content. More importantly, it will help you align solutions with the realities of both learning science and your audience's workflow.

3. **Dig into your compliance requirements.** Why is required training required? Ask questions to get the full background on legacy requirements. Apply modern learning principles where you can to improve the required training experience while checking all the necessary boxes and keeping internal and external stakeholders happy.

4. **Apply a curation mindset.** Maximize your resources by leveraging the absolutely insane amount of content available in the marketplace. Accelerate your speed-to-solution by crowdsourcing content and leveraging external marketplaces. Build when it's the only way to solve the problem.

Last Point

I hope this was a helpful look at the nature of push and pull training within a modern learning ecosystem. Like I said, the entire point of this book is to avoid these layers as much as possible. Structured training will always be a critical part of workplace learning, but it shouldn't be the biggest part of an employee's learning experience.

Now that we've covered the required stuff, let's get on to the most important part of our story: applying the entire MLE Framework to solve a range of workplace learning and performance challenges!

Chapter 9

Applying the MLE Framework

Solve Familiar L&D Problems in New Ways

We're going to do the thing we've only been talking about up until this point. Let's break down the process of applying the Modern Learning Ecosystem Framework to solve workplace performance problems, including:

- How to build audience personas
- How to apply a results-first approach to solution design
- How to decide which layers of the framework to use
- How to shift your learning strategy from programmatic to systematic

We've talked about the idea of implementing a systematic approach to workplace learning. We've detailed the six layers of the MLE Framework. Now let's talk about applying the framework to solve the kinds of problems L&D pros face every day.

It Starts With the Audience

Before jumping into problem-solving mode, you must understand your audience. It's easy to lose sight of what people do day to day when you're dealing with stakeholder requests and lists of skills requirements. When this critical step is overlooked, skills development becomes just another to-do that's easily pushed aside, opportunity gaps emerge, and people fall behind. To provide right-fit solutions, L&D must acknowledge a basic tenant of workplace learning:

> What people learn is determined by their roles, but how
> they learn is influenced by how they work.

You may already have a solid understanding of your audience's workplace experience. Many L&D pros come from the operational side of the business. They worked in the roles they now support. I was a frontline employee and operational manager before I went into L&D with a frontline focus. However, some L&D people are hired in from the outside for their domain expertise but have never worked within the specific industry before. Plus, even those who have done the jobs themselves may be several years removed from the day-to-day reality. With the pace of change in today's workplace, industries go through dramatic transformations in just a few years.

Get to know your audience by immersing yourself in their workflows. Engage employees in regular conversations about their roles. Conduct focus groups, site visits, and surveys to better understand how work gets done. After I moved into L&D with Disney, I regularly picked up shifts within the operation to keep myself grounded. It was always fun to put the costumes back on and interact with guests at The Great Movie Ride or Big Thunder Mountain Railroad. It also helped me understand the challenges cast members faced and how I could potentially help.

This collective insight will help you shape the personas you need to design right-fit solutions using the MLE Framework. Personas are not the same as roles or titles. A large company may have thousands of job codes, making it impossible to consider every individual role when designing your learning ecosystem. The goal is to provide an equitable learning and support experience for every employee, but your ecosystem must also function at scale despite your resource and time constraints. Therefore, it's critical that you focus on personas rather than job titles when applying your framework.

A *persona* is a set of shared characteristics that help you better understand and support a group of people. It's a powerful way to keep operational realities top of mind and focus on the person (not the employee) you're supporting. When building personas to represent your audiences, consider the following attributes:

- **Function:** Does this person work independently or directly with your company's customers and products?
- **Foundation:** Was this person hired for a specific skill set or do they need to learn the basics of how to do their job?
- **Scale:** Does this person have a unique role or do they share their workload?
- **Time:** Does this person have autonomy or is their workload heavily managed?
- **Location:** Where does this person do their work?
- **Access:** How does this person access learning and support resources within the workflow?
- **Motivation:** Is this person focused on meeting foundational job requirements or long-term career goals?
- **Measurement:** Are this person's performance outcomes determined by subjective or objective measures?

As you shape your personas, you will quickly realize that many roles share attributes. For example, delivery drivers, contact center agents, and manufacturing workers do very different jobs. However, they are all heavily scheduled, leverage workflow-based technology, and are held accountable to objective metrics. Your company may have thousands of job codes but only a few dozen unique personas. Focusing on how work is done instead of the work itself makes building an enterprise ecosystem to meet everyone's needs infinitely more manageable.

Map Your Ecosystem

Now that you understand your audience, you must align each persona to the MLE Framework. This is how you will ensure each persona has access to the right tools and resources within your learning ecosystem.

Many learning ecosystems are currently out of balance. Certain layers of the framework are strong while others are weak. The organization may have robust formal training programs but limited tools for knowledge sharing and performance support. Furthermore, these resources may not apply equitably to every persona within the workplace. Corporate employees may use Microsoft Teams to get questions answered by subject matter experts in real time while frontline retail associates are forced to rely on the person next to them, who may or may not be an actual SME.

Use Table 9-1 to list the tactics available to each persona within each layer of your existing learning ecosystem. Note any overlaps where the same tactics apply equitably to different personas. Highlight any clear gaps that exist.

Table 9-1. Example of Availability Gaps Between Personas

Persona	Frontline Employee	Corporate Employee
Shared Knowledge	Wiki	Wiki
Performance Support	—	MS Teams
Reinforcement	Microlearning App	—
Coaching	—	Chat Bot
Pull Training	—	LXP Content Library
Push Training	LMS	LMS

In some cases, you can immediately close the gaps you identify. In the frontline vs. corporate persona example, you could use your LXP-based content library to provide on-demand development opportunities to frontline workers by building mobile-friendly learning paths focused on relevant skills. In other cases, you may need to build up parts of your ecosystem for specific personas over time. For instance, it may take time to identify right-fit tactics that will close your performance support gap within the frontline workforce.

Once you've identified the available tactics within each layer of your framework, it's time to start solving problems.

Identify Your Solution Requirements

The MLE Framework is built to address any workplace performance challenge, regardless of industry, use case, or persona. The same steps apply regardless of the tools or technologies available within your ecosystem. The solutioning process always starts in the same place: the end (Figure 9-1).

Figure 9-1. The Results-First Model for Learning Solution Design

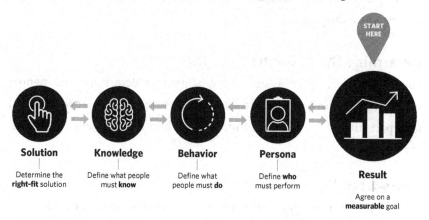

Identify the Measurable Result

You must know where you're going before you map the road to get there. Work with your stakeholders to determine the desired outcome of your learning solution. Start by asking how they determined there was a problem in the first place. This will help identify the clear, measurable result you must agree upon before progressing any further.

Let's use safety training as an example.

A stakeholder comes to L&D with a request to "improve the company's safety culture." L&D immediately recognizes this goal as neither clear nor measurable. They engage the stakeholder in a detailed conversation about the origins of their request, probing for metrics that reveal a proven safety problem. The stakeholder identifies a high lost time incident rate (LTIR, along with data showing the most common workplace injuries over the past three years. L&D narrows the conversation to these proof points, specifically the most common source of lost time injuries: back strains. The stakeholder agrees to focus on reducing back injuries as the first step toward improving their workplace safety program.

"Improving safety culture" is a huge objective with lots of potential points of failure. "Reducing back injuries" is a specific, measurable goal that can be solutioned quickly and accurately. Once L&D proves their ability to solve this initial problem, they can work with the stakeholder to apply the same process to other priority safety topics. If resources permit, this may even happen simultaneously as a parallel workstream to accelerate the project.

Determine the Audience Persona

You know the desired result. Now, you must determine the people involved in making that result a reality. Identify the audience that will take part in your learning solution and outline their persona attributes (Table 9-2).

Table 9-2. Defining the Persona

The back injuries are occurring within the company's distribution warehouses. Therefore, the audience for this solution must include warehouse workers as well as their managers.

Function	Employees work in teams to organize product shipments.
Foundation	Employees have limited experience and are trained to execute required job responsibilities in a safety-critical environment.
Scale	This role is held by 5,000 employees across a network of 18 distribution centers.
Time	Employees are heavily managed with minimal open time during their shifts and have no opportunity to complete work tasks while off-shift.
Location	Employees spend most of their time on the warehouse floor. Breaks are taken in a central break room.
Access	Employees have limited access to technology while working, including kiosks in the break room.
Motivation	Employees are focused on hitting operational metrics, specifically productivity goals, during each shift.
Measurement	Employees are measured based on productivity as well as reduction in safety incidents.

Define the Observable Behavior

You know who will play a key role in achieving the desired business result. Now you must determine how they will make this happen. Defining the on-the-job behaviors required to achieve your result is the most critical part of the solutioning process. It requires you to dig in with your stakeholder and determine if changing employee behavior will actually solve the problem.

L&D discusses the common causes of back injuries within the logistics operation with their stakeholders. They also review incident reports and conduct observations to identify behavior gaps within real-world job performance. L&D finds the majority of back injuries occur when employees improperly lift heavy objects within the workflow. They note that necessary safety equipment is available and point to specific lifting behaviors, such as bending at the knees and keeping arms close to the body, as the primary behavior changes required to achieve the desired result.

In this example, L&D found specific behaviors that must be addressed. However, before making this conclusion, a deep assessment of the job experience will help you make sure that the problem is actually a performance issue that could be addressed with a learning solution. If you had found important safety equipment was unavailable when injuries occurred, this information would have allowed you to push back on stakeholders to close this gap before progressing any further with a learning solution.

Once the observable behaviors are defined, L&D must ask one more question before moving to the next step: Why aren't employees executing these behaviors on the job right now? The answer will determine if a learning solution has the potential to solve this performance problem. For example, if you find out that poor behavior is the result of factors like misaligned expectations, lack of accountability, or limited motivation, you should suggest an alternative solution and not attempt to address the issue with training.

Define the Required Knowledge

You know what employees have to do to achieve the desired result. Now you must determine what they have to know to execute the right behaviors. Your stakeholders and SMEs likely came prepared for this conversation, and they fully believe employees must memorize every word included in their 300-slide PowerPoint presentation. You know otherwise, but you need your stakeholder to agree.

Start with the behaviors you need employees to execute to achieve your desired result. Then, list the specific information points employees need to know to do those things on the job. Qualify each point by repeatedly asking your stakeholder the same question: Could an employee execute the required behavior without knowing this information? If they say no, then the information should be included in your learning solution. If the answer is yes, then the information should be set aside as an extra detail (but not necessarily discarded).

L&D identified safe lifting as a critical behavior for reducing back injuries. Working with their SMEs, they listed the required knowledge points related to safe lifting, including:

- How to execute the steps of a safe lift
- How to properly use safety equipment while executing a lift
- How to identify potential strain or injury
- How to prepare for physically strenuous job activities
- How and when to report a workplace injury

This step focuses your learning solution on just the knowledge needed to solve the problem. However, your stakeholders and SMEs may not agree with the idea of cutting out big chunks of their beloved source information. Don't worry! The MLE Framework includes options like shared knowledge for making sure all 300 slides get covered if absolutely necessary.

Architect Your Solution

You now have all the information you'll need to design a right-fit learning solution. Plus, by connecting the dots between your solution and the desired business result, you've identified the data needed to measure the impact of your solution. Results-first design also provides the foundation for measuring the impact of learning solutions (Figure 9-2).

Figure 9-2. Results-First Design and Measurement

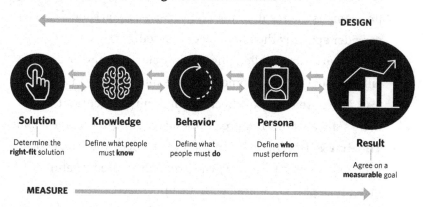

DESIGN

Solution	Knowledge	Behavior	Persona	Result
Determine the **right-fit** solution	Define what people must **know**	Define what people must **do**	Define **who** must perform	Agree on a **measurable** goal

MEASURE

The process for creating a modern learning solution always begins in the same place: the bottom of the framework. Your first move is to determine the shared knowledge component of your solution. How will people access information on-demand for this topic moving forward? Then, move up the framework and apply right-fit tactics from each layer. The framework is designed so that each layer makes the layers above it stronger in application. However, only go up as far as you need to solve the problem. Many of your solutions will therefore not include tactics from the uppermost layers, such as pull and push training, while every solution will include the foundational layers, including shared knowledge and performance support.

There's no exact formula for determining how far up the framework you should go to solve any given performance problem. That said, here are four factors you should consider when creating a modern learning solution:

- **Context.** When and where does your audience need help? Some tactics are better suited for specific workplace environments. For example, a job aid (shared knowledge) is easier to consume in the flow of work on a manufacturing line than an e-learning module (push or pull training).
- **Criticality.** How problematic is failure as related to this topic? If someone can learn through experience and solve their own problems without adding considerable risk to the business, then you may be able to focus on the lower layers of the framework.

However, if someone will get hurt or create major workplace problems as the result of poor performance, you should consider applying the upper layers as well.

- **Complexity.** How challenging is this topic to master? Are we talking about basic customer service skills or flying an Airbus 350? There are plenty of checklists in an airplane cockpit, but there's still a lot of structured training required to become a pilot.
- **Timeliness.** How quickly is a solution needed? Your stakeholder probably wants it yesterday. The lower layers are by nature faster to deploy compared with the upper layers, which require more instructional design and content development effort.

Weigh each of these factors against the performance problem you're trying to solve.

For example, a customer service challenge may have high timeliness (solution desired immediately), low complexity (simple behavior changes), and low criticality (limited risk to the business). Therefore, a solution that includes tactics from only the shared knowledge and performance support layers of your framework may be sufficient to address the issue (Figure 9-3). Context will then help you determine how to provide this solution in a way that best fits your target audience.

Figure 9-3. Only Foundational Layers Applied in Customer Service Solution Example

On the other hand, a problem related to workplace safety, like the example in this chapter, may have high timeliness (solution required immediately), low complexity (simple processes to be executed), and high criticality (high risk to people and the business). Therefore, your solution may include tactics from every layer of the framework (Figure 9-4). However, you should still begin the process at the foundation and determine how shared knowledge and performance support tactics will work alongside more structured elements, such as push and pull training, coaching, and reinforcement. This holistic approach transforms learning from a one-and-done experience to an ongoing support strategy focused on enabling real-world performance.

Figure 9-4. Full Framework Applied in Safety Solution Example

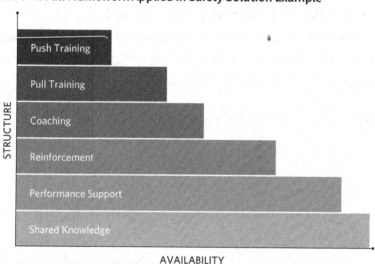

A modern learning ecosystem also enables L&D to build and deploy iterative solutions rather than relying on campaign or project-based approaches. You can deploy right-fit tactics within each framework layer independently when it makes sense based on the needs of your audience. For example, you can publish shared knowledge resources, such as wiki articles, explainer videos, and job aids, to get foundational information into people's hands quickly while still taking the time needed to build a formal training program. Furthermore, when people have a clear understanding regarding how tactics are systematically used within the workflow, you can pulse information to your audience instead of always waiting for every last detail to be finalized. You can publish part of a wiki article along with a note regarding upcoming information to give people the opportunity to participate in the change process as opposed to being impacted by it all at once.

We'll apply the MLE Framework in detail to solve a collection of familiar workplace learning and performance challenges in the next chapter, including returning to the safety example we just explored. For now, remember that the goal is to deliver the simplest, fastest, most accessible and impactful solution possible.

Transform the Learning Experience

Traditional workplace learning is programmatic (Figure 9-5). L&D pushes content and activities at employees in hopes they'll take advantage of these resources to improve their skills and achieve organizational goals.

Figure 9-5. Traditional Push Training Strategy

The MLE Framework restores balance to the workplace learning experience by enabling support tactics within the workflow (Figure 9-6). Employees can easily pull the resources needed to solve timely problems or explore additional development opportunities. They also have learning and support activities pushed to them based on proven performance gaps and organizational priorities. Programmatic learning doesn't go away. It just becomes the exception as opposed to the rule. Plus, continuous learning tactics like shared knowledge and reinforcement improve the impact of programmatic solutions by allowing designers to focus on what matters most rather than attempting to pack every possible piece of information into a single piece of content.

Figure 9-6. Traditional Strategy Augmented With Continuous Learning Tactics

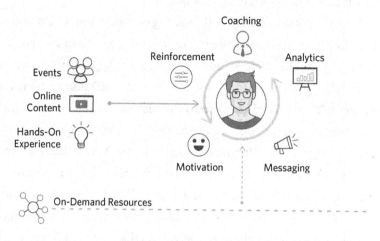

The strategic combination of programmatic and systematic learning tactics fosters sustained knowledge growth, targeted business results, and a collaborative learning culture in which the rising tide of capability raises all boats. Employees receive a balanced learning and support experience so they can solve today's problems while building the skills needed to be successful in the future (Figure 9-7).

Figure 9-7. Continuous Learning Experience

As Clark Quinn Once Said

Clark Quinn inspired me to think differently about my work when he said "JD, you're funnier on Twitter than you are in person."

Wait . . . that's the wrong Clark Quinn quote. Although I still don't know if that was a compliment or not.

During another equally enlightening conversation, Clark said to me: "Our job is to do the least work possible to accomplish our goal." That sounds lazy on the surface, but it's really a strategic way to think about architecting modern learning solutions. Every L&D function has limited resources. Therefore, these resources must be focused on the issues that matter most to the people and organizations we support so L&D can have the biggest possible impact. When we don't have the right systems in place, it's easy to get distracted by low value training requests that consume a huge chunk of our resources. The MLE Framework and its results-first design principles keep L&D pros focused on the behaviors, knowledge, and tactics that help people do their best work, regardless of the challenge they're currently facing.

Chapter 10

MLE in Action

Explore Five Examples of the Framework in Practice

Let's do the thing! We're going to apply the MLE Framework in a series of real-world scenarios so you can see how the pieces fit together to form holistic learning and support solutions.

The previous chapter explained how to apply the Modern Learning Ecosystem Framework in concept. Now, let's do it for real! Here are five examples of how the framework can be used to solve real-world performance problems.

Note: The following examples are based on real-world projects. Details have been adjusted, omitted, or simplified to make each story more clear, relevant, and lawyer-friendly. I've also replaced company names with some of my favorite pop culture brands to add even more fun to our already jovial learning strategy conversation.

Example 1: Warehouse Safety at Buy'n'Large

Let's finish the story we started in the previous chapter about injury prevention in a network of warehouses.

The Problem

A safety manager approached L&D with a request to "improve the safety culture" within the logistics operation. Given how large and nondescript this request was from the start, L&D applied the MLE Framework to identify the specific problem to be addressed as well as the right-fit solution.

Measurable Result: Reduce LTIR by 15%

L&D collaborated with stakeholders to identify the most common cause of workplace injuries within the logistics network: back strains. As a first step to improving the overall workplace safety culture, L&D targeted an achievable reduction in lost time incident rate (LTIR) of 15 percent over the next six months.

Audience: Frontline Warehouse Workers

L&D conducted a workplace experience assessment to outline the persona attributes for the frontline warehouse worker.

- **Function:** Employees work in large teams to organize product shipments within the warehouse environment.
- **Foundation:** Employees usually have limited experience and are trained to execute core job responsibilities in a safety-critical environment.
- **Scale:** This work is done by 5,000 employees across a network of 18 distribution centers.
- **Time:** Employees are heavily managed with minimal open time during their shifts.
- **Location:** Employees spend most of their time on the warehouse floor with breaks taken in a central break room.
- **Access:** Employees have limited access to technology while working, including kiosks in the break room. Most training

materials are only available in English, regardless of workers' primary languages.

- **Motivation:** employees are focused on hitting operational metrics, specifically productivity goals during each shift.
- **Measurement:** Employees are measured with a range of productivity and safety metrics.

Observable Behavior: Execute a Safe Lift

L&D reviewed incident reports, conducted observations, and spoke with frontline workers and managers about the common causes of back injuries. They determined the majority of back injuries occurred when employees improperly lifted heavy objects. L&D noted the necessary safety equipment was available and being used consistently. Related work considerations, such as productivity metrics and environment, did not appear to contribute to the performance challenge. This pointed them toward common flaws in the lifting process, including failure to bend at the knees and to keep arms close to the body.

Required Knowledge

Frontline warehouse workers need to know:

- How to execute the steps of a safe lift
- How to properly use safety equipment while executing a lift
- How to identify potential strain or injury
- How to prepare for physically strenuous job activities
- How and when to report a workplace injury

L&D collaborated with stakeholders and subject matter experts within the safety function to identify the knowledge points required to execute a safe lift. They noted this information was included in new hire training for all warehouse workers. However, this information was not consistently available or reinforced after the initial training period.

Right-Fit Considerations

L&D considered four factors—context, criticality, complexity, and timeliness—when using the MLE Framework to craft a solution.

- **Context: Operational.** Employees must recall and apply knowledge related to safe lifting within their workflow on the warehouse floor.
- **Criticality: High.** Poor performance is resulting in employee injuries, compensation claims, and lost time disruptions.
- **Complexity: Low.** Executing a safe lift is not difficult if the correct steps are followed and precautions are taken. Workers are selected and assigned to their responsibilities based on their ability to perform this type of work.
- **Timeliness: High.** People are currently at risk of injury if they do not execute the necessary safety behaviors.

The Solution

After reviewing all the information, L&D used the MLE Framework to build a solution.

Shared Knowledge: Safe Lifting Guides

Visual guides detailing the steps in a safe lift were posted in parts of the warehouse where these behaviors are most commonly applied. These guides were also translated into a selection of languages that reflect the workforce.

Video demonstrations of safe lifting behaviors featuring real warehouse workers were developed and posted on the company intranet for on-demand access. The videos were produced in English with subtitles available in additional languages.

Performance Support: Team Safety Champions

Employees with proven safety records were designated as team champions. Management ensured that at least one champion was working during every shift so they could act as a go-to resource and peer coach for any employees who needed help.

Reinforcement: Question-Based Reinforcement

All warehouse employees received digital reinforcement training at the start of every shift. Each session took less than three minutes to complete and included three multiple choice questions on safe lifting practices. Employees accessed this reinforcement using kiosks in the break room.

Coaching: Leading Indicator Insight

Frontline managers conducted behavior observations on the warehouse floor during every shift using company-issued tablets. This data was combined with results from ongoing reinforcement training to provide managers with leading indicators of potential safety risks. Managers could then conduct coaching conversations with employees who demonstrated low knowledge levels or poor job performance before injuries occurred.

Pull Training

L&D determined that pull training wasn't necessary.

Push Training

L&D determined that push training wasn't necessary.

The Result

Few workplace topics are as serious as safety training. No one wants people to get hurt on the job. It's easy to default to traditional, course-based training as part of safety interventions. However, even the most serious topics require a right-fit solution. Safety may also be the most behavior-specific workplace topic, as simple mistakes and shortcuts can have massive consequences. Therefore, it's even more important for L&D to follow a consistent process to connect on-the-job behavior to impactful support and measurable results.

This logistics operation recorded a 50 percent reduction in LTIR over a six-month period, far exceeding their initial goal. They achieved this result without removing employees from the operation for formal training activities. The safety elements within new hire training were found to be accurate and consistent with the new reinforcement and support tactics. The results and positive feedback garnered during this project served as a meaningful first step towards the reinvigoration of the company's safety culture.

Example 2: Retail Loss Prevention at Quick Stop

The Problem
The VP of store operations approached L&D with a request to retrain all retail associates in loss prevention due to an ongoing increase in inventory shrink. The company was experiencing seven-figure losses annually due to customer and employee theft across their US store network.

Measurable Result: Reduce Shrink Rate by 30%
L&D collaborated with stakeholders to identify the best metric to target related to loss prevention challenges within the retail store network. They arrived at an achievable reduction in shrink rate (lost retail value of merchandise) of 30 percent over the next year.

Audience: Retail Store Associates
L&D conducted a workplace experience assessment to outline the persona attributes for the retail store associate.

- **Function:** Employees work in small teams to complete all frontline functions within retail stores.
- **Foundation:** Employees have limited experience, including many working their first jobs, and are trained to execute core job responsibilities.
- **Scale:** This work is done by 15,000 employees across a store network with 1,000 locations.
- **Time:** Employees are customer-facing and have limited extra time during their shifts.
- **Location:** Employees do most of their work on the retail sales floor with minimal time spent back of house.
- **Access:** Employees use a single terminal as a point of sale, time clock, and intranet portal.
- **Motivation:** Employees are focused on short-term operational goals, including product sales and customer satisfaction.

- **Measurement:** Employees are measured based on operational results, including sales revenue, basket size, loyalty card sign ups, and net promoter score.

Observable Behaviors
- Identify and report potential theft
- Avoid accidental merchandise loss

L&D reviewed loss prevention policies, conducted in-store observations, and met with subject matter experts and retail associates to discuss the realities of retail theft. They determined the primary cause of shrink to be purposeful or accidental theft by customers and employees. Other potential causes, such as inventory mistakes or damaged products, were ruled out.

Required Knowledge
Retail store associates need to understand:
- Loss prevention policy
- Common theft indicators
- Loss prevention practices

L&D collaborated with stakeholders in store operations and loss prevention to identify the knowledge points required to identify and report potential theft. They noted that loss prevention policies and tactics were included in the employee handbook and new hire associate training. However, this information was not regularly covered after the first two days on the job.

Right-Fit Considerations
L&D considered four factors—context, criticality, complexity, and timeliness—when using the MLE Framework to craft a solution.
- **Context: Operational.** Employees work across a network of small stores with limited staffing and cannot be removed from the operation for extended periods. Deploying trainers to deliver classroom sessions in every store would be expensive and take months to complete.

- **Criticality: High.** Shrink is an expensive problem. It's not resulting in major risks to employees or customers, but it is costing the business a lot of money that must be recouped in other areas.
- **Complexity: Low.** Shrink is a straight-forward problem that requires the right level of attention and preventative action.
- **Timeliness: High.** This is an escalating issue that is costing the company money every day.

The Solution

After reviewing all the information, L&D used the MLE Framework to build a solution.

Shared Knowledge: Loss Prevention Policy and Practices

The existing loss prevention guidelines were rewritten to be more straightforward and actionable while limiting legalese. This content was added to the company intranet as a searchable asset separate from the larger employee handbook.

Performance Support: Loss Prevention Hotline

The company already had a loss prevention hotline that most employees did not know about. Contact information was posted in working areas, including cash wraps and storage rooms.

Reinforcement: Loss Prevention Scenarios

All retail associates received reinforcement training at the start of each shift. After clocking in on the point-of-sale computer, they received two scenario-based questions about theft prevention. The questions increased in difficulty over time as associates demonstrated their knowledge of the topic.

Coaching

L&D determined that coaching wasn't necessary.

Pull Training

L&D determined that pull training wasn't necessary.

Push Training

L&D determined that push training wasn't necessary.

The Result

Retail training is always a question of scale and capacity. How can a small corporate L&D team enable behavior change and performance improvement across a massive store network, especially when employees are focused on serving customers and don't sit in front of computers all day? This project demonstrated the importance of architecting a workplace learning system that fits the day-to-day reality of the audience. When people can't break away from work for extended learning activities, L&D must shift their approach and provide solutions that can be easily accessed within the workflow.

This retailer reduced their shrink rate by over 60 percent within the first year of their learning initiative. Associates were able to access all learning resources while on the sales floor, thereby avoiding any disruption to the operation and maintaining the focus on customer service and sales execution. The company subsequently expanded their use of these learning tactics to address other frontline performance challenges, including sales processes, customer service practices, and product knowledge.

Example 3: Product Training at Meta Cortex

The Problem

The director of operations approached L&D with a request to improve the product knowledge of their contact center agents. The organization determined that product specialization was the best way to improve customer service. Rather than require agents to understand all the company's products, employees would instead be grouped into teams that focused on specific product lines. Customer calls would then be routed to specialized agents to ensure quick and knowledgeable service.

Measurable Result: Increase First Call Resolution by 50%

L&D collaborated with stakeholders to identify the best metric related to their operational goal of improving customer service. Of the robust data set available within the contact center, first call resolution was identified as a major contributor to customer satisfaction and ongoing intent to buy. L&D arrived at an aggressive but achievable target to increase first call resolution by 50 percent over the next two fiscal quarters.

Audience: Contact Center Agents

L&D conducted a workplace experience assessment to outline the persona attributes for the contact center agent.

- **Function:** Agents work independently within small teams to support inbound and outbound service calls.
- **Foundation:** Agents have varying degrees of experience in contact center operations and limited depth of experience with the company's products, which are constantly changing.
- **Scale:** This work is done by 800 agents across five domestic contact centers, including a small group of work from home agents.
- **Time:** Agents are managed to the minute to ensure appropriate staffing and limited call wait times.
- **Location:** Agents work at desks on the contact center floor or remotely from home offices.

- **Access:** Agents use desktop computers and multiple applications to manage customer information, make and receive calls, and access job-related information.
- **Motivation:** Agents are focused on short-term operational goals, especially those that directly affect their compensation.
- **Measurement:** Agents are measured on a range of contact center metrics, including first call resolution, hold time, quality assessment, and net promoter score.

Observable Behaviors

- Promptly identify the root cause of a customer problem
- Troubleshoot the customer problem to identify the appropriate solution
- Accurately respond to customer questions about products and services

L&D reviewed call quality reports, listened to call recordings, shadowed agents during live calls, and spoke with contact center managers and agents. They saw that the successful agents could promptly identify the root cause of a customer's problem. They determined the primary cause of repeat and transferred customer calls to be poor troubleshooting execution due to limited product and process knowledge.

Required Knowledge

Call center representatives need to understand:

- Foundational product knowledge
- How to troubleshoot common customer problems
- How to use reference materials during customer calls

L&D collaborated with product and call quality managers to identify the knowledge points required to effectively troubleshoot customer problems. They noted that much of this knowledge is continuously changing as products and processes are updated. Agents practice this behavior during new hire training but are then expected to keep up with and apply changes announced via email communication and team huddles.

Right-Fit Considerations

L&D considered four factors—context, criticality, complexity, and timeliness—when using the MLE Framework to craft a solution.

- **Context: Operational.** Agent time is heavily managed to ensure proper staffing for anticipated call volume. Since contact centers experience high turnover, extra staffing is typically not available. This means that agents cannot be removed from the phones unless absolutely necessary.
- **Criticality: Low.** Customer service is a strategic priority for the business, but the reorganization that created this project is proactive in nature and not due to any major business problems.
- **Complexity: High.** The product and process knowledge required to execute the desired behaviors are not complex. However, the pace with which this information changes adds considerable complexity to the agent workflow and must therefore be addressed within the solution.
- **Timeliness: High.** The operations team wants to begin reorganizing agents and routing calls based on product specialization as soon as possible.

The Solution

After reviewing all the information, L&D used the MLE Framework to build a solution.

Shared Knowledge

- Product Wiki Pages
- Troubleshooting Process Guides
- Call Recording Library
- Business Update Summary Posts

A wiki was already being used to house all critical job information for agents. L&D partnered with product managers to build pages for each product. They also provided consistent page templates, which were then filled in and maintained by product managers to ensure timely updates. Pages were built to feature the most commonly referenced information first, followed by more granular details. The pages replaced the PDF product data sheets that were traditionally distributed by product managers via email.

L&D partnered with product managers and agents to build troubleshooting guides related to each product. These guides used decision trees to walk agents through the process of resolving common customer issues.

L&D partnered with quality managers to build a library of exemplary calls for each product. This library was housed within the call evaluation platform, and links were added to the product pages within the wiki for easy access. Quality managers continuously updated the library as part of their evaluation process.

L&D introduced a new section of the wiki dedicated to business update summaries. A curator within the operations team maintained a list of all product and process updates. They then published a post at the end of each week highlighting these changes by sharing links to related wiki articles. The posts were also organized by product so agents could quickly identify updates relevant to their roles.

Performance Support: Product Page Comments

The wiki being used as the company knowledge base included threaded commenting within each article. L&D leveraged this feature as a performance support tool to answer questions related to products and services. L&D community managers would either answer questions themselves or mention subject matter experts, who received email notifications and were then responsible for providing the requested information.

Over time, agents and SMEs started answering questions on their own, and the L&D community managers were phased out.

Reinforcement: Troubleshooting Scenarios

L&D developed a series of multiple-choice scenarios focused on troubleshooting common customer problems. These scenarios were used as daily reinforcement training for agents. In addition, agents were assigned training tasks within the contact center operations software at the beginning of their shifts and after returning from scheduled breaks. The task was linked to a reinforcement activity in the LMS, which the agent then spent three minutes completing before returning to their call queue.

Coaching: Call Assessment Rubrics

L&D partnered with quality managers to build new assessment rubrics for contact center managers. These rubrics focused on behaviors related to troubleshooting and product knowledge, which managers then used to evaluate three calls per week and enter qualitative and quantitative observations into the quality system. This data was then used to inform coaching conversations and personalize ongoing agent training.

Pull Training

L&D determined that pull training wasn't necessary.

Push Training: Product Specialization Paths

L&D blended a combination of assets, including wiki pages, call recordings, and scenarios, to create specialized training paths within the LMS. Each path included both knowledge and performance assessments for completion.

These paths provided a structured product training experience for new agents during onboarding. They were also used to cross-train agents into new specializations as managers shifted people between teams to meet changing customer demand.

The Result

Contact centers are the most difficult office-based learning environments for one simple reason: People must stay on the phone. This heavily restricts L&D options, despite the ease with which agents can be reached via technology. In this case, L&D also heavily relied on product managers for resource development and ongoing updates. L&D turned these challenges into opportunities by releasing resources as they were developed rather than pushing a full program that agents would not have time to complete anyway.

Once the full complement of resources was made available, the contact center quickly saw improvements in first call resolution. They achieved the aggressive 50 percent reduction goal within six months of starting the project. The resource-based approach was especially important moving forward, as management made continuous changes to team structures and specialization requirements. Their decision to build product-specific assets in partnership with SMEs and avoid long-form courses made it much easier for L&D to keep pace with operational changes. It also established a model for addressing other performance challenges within the time-limited, execution-focused contact center environment.

Example 4: Management Coaching at Thunder Bifflin

The Problem

Senior management approached L&D with a request for training to improve the coaching delivered by sales managers. The company was experiencing a decline in revenue, especially among less experienced sales professionals. Senior management started looking for ways to improve performance. They restructured the sales process and invested in new customer relationship management and enablement technologies. But they wanted to be sure managers had the skills needed to support this strategy and therefore requested L&D support.

Measurable Result: Improve Coaching Index Scores by 30%

L&D asked stakeholders to explain the relationship between coaching and sales execution. They requested evidence to verify the assumption that existing coaching behaviors were ineffective, but stakeholders were unable to provide a quantitative measure. Nonetheless, stakeholders they remained stalwart in their request for a learning solution.

L&D worked with stakeholders to devise a new measurement strategy for coaching. L&D designed a series of 360-degree feedback mechanisms, including team member surveys, knowledge assessments, and coaching observation forms. The resulting data was combined to give each manager a coaching index score.

L&D then used these measurement tools to conduct an assessment of existing manager behaviors. After 30 days, they analyzed the data to arrive at a baseline and then worked with stakeholders to determine an achievable goal to improve this result by 30 percent over the next quarter.

Audience: Sales Managers

L&D conducted a workplace experience assessment to outline the persona attributes for the sales manager:

- **Function:** Managers supported small teams of sales professionals in their daily execution.

- **Foundation:** Most managers were previously high-performing sales professionals who were then promoted into their current roles with limited people management experience.
- **Scale:** This work is done by 40 managers, each supporting a team of 10 to 15 sales professionals.
- **Time:** Managers have significant autonomy over how they run their teams within an established process.
- **Location:** Managers are mobile, working from the office, home, and on the road supporting sales efforts. Some have minimal in-person contact with their team members.
- **Access:** Managers use company-provided laptops and smartphones for all work functions.
- **Motivation:** Managers are focused on short-term sales goals, which heavily impact their job status and compensation.
- **Measurement:** Managers are measured based on quarterly sales targets and ongoing pipeline management.

Observable Behaviors
- Consistently completing coaching pre-work
- Asking effective probing questions to determine root causes of performance gaps
- Solving coaching problems in collaboration with peers

L&D reviewed the results of the coaching index assessment. They spoke with managers with high and low index scores and observed as they engaged in coaching conversations. In some cases, they recorded these interactions for further review.

L&D identified a set of key behaviors that were consistently applied by managers with high index scores but rarely or never applied by those with low scores. This included reviewing a team member's metrics and other relevant information before the coaching conversation, digging in to identify the true cause of performance gaps before making recommendations, and partnering with other managers to overcome particularly challenging problems.

L&D also reviewed sales reports to determine the connection between revenue outcomes and coaching index scores. They found that managers with higher index scores tended to also record better sales results. However, several managers with low index scores also consistently achieved their sales goals.

Required Knowledge

Sales managers need to know:

- How to access and analyze sales performance data
- How to prioritize coaching conversation topics
- How to ask effective probing questions
- How to set mutually agreed-upon goals
- When to seek help from peers

L&D collaborated with sales managers with proven coaching capabilities to identify the knowledge points required to effectively execute the desired behavior set. They noted that much of this information was covered during training for high-potential sales team members. However, it was not reintroduced or reinforced once a salesperson was promoted into a manager role.

Right-Fit Considerations

L&D considered four factors—context, criticality, complexity, and timeliness—when using the MLE Framework to craft a solution.

- **Context: Embedded.** Sales managers are constantly on the go supporting sales deals. They spend most of their time in meetings with team members and prospects. Some regularly meet with their teams in-person while others engage virtually with remote and traveling direct reports. If a task isn't directly related to their ability to close a deal and hit a KPI, they are unlikely to engage.
- **Criticality: Low.** Analysis showed that managers are able to hit sales targets regardless of coaching execution. However, it also revealed the potential to reach even better outcomes with improved coaching.

- **Complexity: High.** Having a quality, actionable coaching conversation is difficult, especially for managers with limited experience and virtual team members. Providing right-fit support tools may reduce this complexity.
- **Timeliness: High.** Stakeholders are pushing for a timely solution, regardless of proven business impact.

The Solution

After reviewing all the information, L&D used the MLE Framework to build a solution.

Shared Knowledge: Proven Practice Articles and Videos

L&D worked with managers who demonstrated effective coaching behaviors to build user generated content in the company's shared knowledge base. These articles included proven practices for executing a quality coaching session as well as tips for overcoming common challenges. L&D also produced a series of videos featuring sales managers explaining more nuanced coaching concepts. These videos were embedded within the related articles to provide a one-stop shop for coaching information.

Performance Support

- Coaching Champions
- Collaboration Sessions
- Manager Q&A Channel

L&D worked with senior management to designate select managers as coaching champions. They acted as go-to resources for managers struggling with their coaching behaviors. Champions roles were voluntary and reviewed on an annual basis.

L&D scheduled a series of monthly virtual collaboration sessions. These roundtable conversations provided managers with a dedicated opportunity to ask questions of their peers. L&D promoted these sessions via email and facilitated conversations on specific coaching topics.

A dedicated channel within the company's chat platform was also created for manager topics, including coaching. Coaching champions received notifications when managers submitted questions, and L&D ensured all inquiries were answered in a timely manner.

Reinforcement

- Practice Scenarios
- Practice Session Calendar

L&D developed a series of multiple-choice practice scenarios focused on desired coaching behaviors. Managers received nudge communications via chat messages with the goal of completing at least one scenario in the LMS every week.

In addition, L&D published a calendar of one-on-one coaching practice sessions. They developed a series of coaching scenario scripts and trained L&D and coaching champions to execute practice sessions. Managers could voluntarily sign up for practice sessions, and L&D handled the scheduling logistics.

Coaching: Coaching Index Reviews

L&D worked with senior management to sustain the coaching index measurement process. Team members received anonymous monthly surveys inquiring about their coaching experiences. Senior managers completed a minimum of three coaching observations per month, initially with guidance from L&D to ensure consistent expectations. These metrics were combined with data from ongoing reinforcement activities to provide an updated coaching index for each manager, which appeared on the senior manager's CRM dashboard.

Senior managers used this index and related data points during their monthly check-ins with each sales manager. If a manager executed specific coaching behaviors well, the senior manager recommended they share their insights via proven practice articles. If they struggled with certain behaviors, the senior manager recommended they take advantage of the provided support resources, including collaboration sessions, one-on-one practice, and OTS courses.

Pull Training: OTS Coaching Courses

L&D leveraged an existing subscription with an OTS course provider to curate a content path focused on basic coaching behaviors. This was included as an option for managers who received negative feedback during their check-ins.

Push Training

L&D determined that push training wasn't necessary.

The Result

This was an imperfect project from the start. Senior management came to L&D with a vague problem and assumed solution. When L&D was unable to verify the problem due to lack of measurement, stakeholders continued to press for a learning solution. Sometimes it just doesn't matter if you ask the right questions. L&D doesn't always get to decide which projects are worth doing.

However, the L&D team's systematic approach to this project proved invaluable. They were able to close the measurement gap, identify an opportunity to improve performance outcomes, and fulfill their stakeholder's request. The project took longer than anticipated to complete, but it helped shift the organization's perspective on coaching. Once all the pieces were in place, L&D helped management achieve their goal of increasing coaching index scores by 30 percent over a three-month period. Motivated by these results, senior management then integrated the coaching index into the review process for sales managers. Coaching behavior directly affected their compensation, not nearly as much as revenue outcomes of course. This demonstrated the organization's commitment to coaching and validated L&D's data-driven approach to learning and performance.

Example 5: Food Safety Training at Food and Stuff

The Problem

The compliance team came to L&D to execute the annual food safety refresher. Every September, grocery employees were required to complete an online refresher course on basic food safety, including food handling, labeling, and storage. This 30-minute course had been developed internally several years prior and was updated as needed to align with changing regulations. L&D was responsible for administering the process and providing reporting to the compliance team. While content development needs were minimal, the process still required considerable L&D capacity to make sure every associate across the store network completed the training by the 30-day deadline.

Measurable Result

- 100% Completion and Assessment Scores
- 50% Reduction in Administrative Effort

The annual food safety refresher was a check-the-box activity and not intended to change employee behavior. Rather, it provided compliance with the reporting necessary to prove employee competence during regulatory audits.

Checking this box required considerable effort from the L&D and operations teams, given the scale of the frontline workforce. This required initiative pushed L&D resources away from priority work without a clear value proposition. Plus, the refresher training was an internal compliance requirement and not dictated by an external regulator.

Given the number of high-priority projects in the pipeline, L&D decided to find a way to meet compliance requirements (100 percent completion and assessment scores) while reducing administrative effort. At the same time, they also wanted to make sure this mandatory training effort reinforced the desired food safety behaviors.

Audience: Frontline Grocery Associates

L&D conducted a workplace experience assessment to outline the persona attributes for the frontline grocery associate:

- **Function:** Associates work in large teams to execute various functions throughout the grocery operation, including customer service, specialty departments, and back of house roles.
- **Foundation:** Associates typically have limited experience in their roles and are trained to execute core job responsibilities.
- **Scale:** This work is done by 75,000 associates across 500 domestic locations.
- **Time:** Associates are heavily managed, with most of their time spent completing operational tasks.
- **Location:** Associates spend most of their time within their assigned store departments, with breaks taken in a central break room.
- **Access:** Associates use varying technologies as part of their operational work, including point-of-sale systems, scales, handheld devices, and tablets. Personal mobile devices are not permitted for use on the job.
- **Motivation:** Associates are focused on achieving shift-based goals and maximizing their hours to increase earning potential.
- **Measurement:** Associates are measured with a combination of productivity and customer service metrics, such as scans per minute, order fulfillment speed, and net promoter score.

Observable Behaviors

- How to properly handle food
- How to properly label food
- How to properly store food
- How to determine if food is acceptable to use and sell
- How to properly dispose of expired food

L&D reviewed standard operating procedures related to food safety to identify critical job behaviors. They found these behaviors to be part of standard job functions within the stores, which were therefore measured consistently by managers and internal auditors.

Required Knowledge

Frontline grocery associates need to know:

- Food handling guidelines
- Food labeling requirements
- Food storage guidelines
- Food preparation processes
- Food spoilage processes

L&D partnered with store management to identify the knowledge points required to execute tasks associated with food safety. They found most of these processes were documented in standard operating procedures and checklists stored in binders within various store departments. These binders were regularly updated by department managers as procedures changed.

Right-Fit Considerations

L&D considered four factors—context, criticality, complexity, and timeliness—when using the MLE Framework to craft a solution.

- **Context: Operational.** Grocery operations are tightly staffed, and every associate has an assigned role and task list. Therefore, associates cannot be removed from the operation for any extended period of time without disrupting the customer experience. The traditional 30-minute refresh course is an example of this disruption, as associates must be scheduled out of their departments to visit the store training office and complete the course during their shifts. However, because there is a limited number of training computers available in each location, only a few associates may complete the training at any given time throughout the day.
- **Criticality: High.** Food safety is a critical concept within grocery operations. Therefore, any changes to related training and support processes must be thoroughly vetted and approved by all required stakeholders.
- **Complexity: Low.** Associates execute standard, documented processes to ensure all food safety requirements are met.

This work has limited complexity as long as standards are properly followed.

- **Timeliness: Low.** Stakeholders were not searching for a solution to a new problem. They just wanted to execute the same old process. L&D wanted to find a better way to meet compliance requirements while reducing strain on their team and operational partners. Therefore, they could operate on their own timeline as long as they continued to meet compliance requirements.

The Solution

After reviewing all the information, L&D used the MLE Framework to build a solution.

Shared Knowledge: Digital SOPs and Checklists

L&D worked with store management to identify gaps in information access, including the lack of reliability of printed documents in binders. L&D partnered with department managers to digitize all standard operating procedures and checklists within the company's knowledge base. These documents were accessible using any internet-connected device in the store, including POS terminals, handheld devices, and back office computers.

Performance Support: Food Safety Online Community

L&D partnered with department managers to create an online support community related to food safety. Store associates could use this space to ask questions and share proven practices. Department managers were responsible for making sure all questions were answered in a timely manner.

Reinforcement: Reinforcement Questions

L&D repurposed questions from the annual refresher assessment as reinforcement activities. Associates were given the option to answer two questions per shift as part of a gamified learning experience. The points they received for correct answers could be redeemed for prizes such as gift cards and company swag items.

Coaching: Digital Observation and Audit Forms

L&D partnered with department managers to digitize the existing behavior observation and audit forms related to food safety using the company's task management platform. This data was then used to inform ongoing training and coaching initiatives.

Pull Training

L&D determined that pull training wasn't necessary.

Push Training: Refresh Training Course and Assessment

While L&D worked with the compliance team to deliver the annual refresher, they also requested permission to introduce the additional tactics listed within this outline over the following months. Compliance was supportive, as they were getting the boxes they needed checked.

The Result

Getting people to complete one 30-minute online course once per year may sound like an easy task. However, it's not, especially when the audience includes 75,000 full-time and part-time employees across 500 locations. L&D has to review, test, and launch online courses and assessments in multiple languages. Operations managers have to schedule extra staff so associates have time to complete the training. There are also the inevitable login issues and assessment retake requests. Plus, L&D has to generate and distribute reports to every store so managers can hunt down people who haven't completed the training by the due date.

Boxes will always have to be checked but if L&D can find the most efficient ways possible to check them, they can keep their limited capacity focused on the organization's biggest priorities. In this case, L&D leveraged an existing process to introduce long-term change. They still executed the requested check-the-box training, but they surrounded it with additional right-fit tactics.

Over the next year, L&D made it easier for department managers to update procedures using digital tools. They increased the volume and velocity of data collection related to performance behaviors and they used ongoing reinforcement training to measure associates' changing knowledge of job practices.

When it was time for the next refresher training, L&D presented their compliance partners with the improved strategy, including data verifying current knowledge on compliance topics at an organizational, regional, store, department, and associate level. This time around, only locations with subpar knowledge levels were required to complete the 30-minute annual food safety refresher and L&D was able to dramatically reduce the administrative effort required to execute the process.

Putting L&D on Repeat

You may be thinking "All of those stories sound a lot alike." Exactly!

The MLE Framework transforms workplace learning and support into a consistent, repeatable system. The tools, tactics, and technologies organizations use may be different, but the process is always the same. A systems approach helps stakeholders, subject matter experts, managers, and employees understand how learning works within their company—regardless of the topic at hand.

Each story began in the same place: identifying a measurable business result. Then, L&D determined the audience persona, observable behaviors, knowledge requirements, and solution considerations. Finally, L&D executed solutions using only the necessary MLE Framework levels. Every story included shared knowledge and performance support, because every solution should include these elements to make sure employees always have the information they need to do their best work. However, only two of our five stories included push (formal) training. That's because the MLE Framework transforms push training into a last-resort tactic. It doesn't go away. It just gets applied when it's absolutely necessary and always in combination with the layers beneath it on the framework.

I hope these "inspired by real events" stories have made the MLE Framework feel more practical and less theoretical. Give the process a try using one of your recent L&D projects. Work through the various steps from the examples in this chapter and determine how you would have addressed the performance challenge differently using the MLE Framework.

Chapter 11

Making Good Technology Decisions

Use Personas to Build Right-Fit Digital Experiences

We're going to talk about technology and the role it plays within a modern learning ecosystem. This is another one of those topics that should be its own book, so we're going to stick to a few basic ideas, including:

- The seven reasons to apply technology within workplace learning
- How to craft a persona-based digital learning experience
- When to build vs. buy technology
- How to assess the value of learning technology

How many apps do you have on your phone? Unless you're an avid flip phone user, you definitely have more than one. The average US smartphone user had 20 apps installed as of 2019 (Statista). I have 47 on my iPhone as I'm writing this, and that's an all-time low. Most of them hover in the background waiting to be called upon, but I use the 20 on my homescreen as part of my daily routine. For example:

- Safari helps me search for information and keep up with the latest news.
- Slack connects me to my work team through synchronous chat.
- Peloton tracks my daily workouts.

- Axonify reinforces critical knowledge about my job.
- Instacart lets me order groceries from home and schedule pickups.
- Overcast streams podcasts during my morning runs.
- Google Calendar makes sure I'm on time for my next meeting
- YouTube keeps me entertained for a few minutes here and there throughout the day.
- Gmail is . . . Gmail.

These apps have plenty of features and lots of content I don't use, but that doesn't lessen their value. I selected, installed, and positioned each with purpose, and I regularly assess their value as new options emerge. For example, Overcast is at least my 10th podcast app. I like it, but I'm totally willing to swap it out if I find a better alternative.

People manage to use dozens of smartphone apps every day, but they can't figure out which platform to use at work to get timely questions answered. Should they send an email? Maybe they should drop a message on Microsoft Teams? Or is this topic supposed to be solved through the HR system? Unfortunately, employees typically don't get to choose their work tools. This means that the inherent sense of purpose and value they have with their smartphone apps is missing on the job.

This goes for learning technology too. An LMS is just one part of a complex web of digital workplace systems. We can't fix our company's broken tech stack, but we can certainly do our best to avoid adding even more friction to an already prickly user experience. L&D must create a learning technology ecosystem grounded in clear purpose and value. It's time to make learning at work as simple as using a smartphone.

The One Ring Fallacy

Technology is now the face of L&D, with the COVID-19 pandemic forever altering workers' relationships with technology. According to the ATD's *2021 State of the Industry* report, the average number of formal learning hours used via technology-based methods jumped from 41.7 percent in 2018 to 56.1 percent in 2019 to 80.3 percent in 2020. Now, remote and hybrid employees rely on digital tools to access information and connect with peers. For example, 84 percent of organizations in the US use at least one learning management system (Statista). Frontline employees leverage handheld devices, smartphones, and mobile apps to engage with work in new ways. Digital activities are just one part of the workplace learning experience. Tactics like hands-on training, coaching, and classroom sessions also remain important. However, even these parts of the learning experience are more digitally enabled thanks to bots, interaction apps, and interactive guides.

Technology may be a ubiquitous part of work, but that doesn't mean it's getting simpler. Bringing together the right tools to give every employee an equitable experience gets harder as technology evolves and organizations become more complex. In the early 2000s, there were a handful of technology products focused on workplace learning. Today, there are hundreds—each with their own specialties.

The global education technology market was valued at US $89.49 billion in 2020 and is on track to see a compound annual growth rate (CAGR) of 19.9 percent from 2021 to 2028 (Grand View Research 2021). LMS. LXP. Microlearning. Coaching. Assessment. Personalization. Mixed reality. With so many tools available in the marketplace, learning technology often blends into a cacophony of marketing noise and unsubstantiated hype. It's almost impossible to keep up with the latest innovations, even for someone like me whose job is to keep up with the latest innovations. When you spend all your time trying to solve the next big workplace performance problem, how can you really tell if the latest and greatest is actually the latest and greatest?

L&D teams only have so much time to explore new learning technology and so much money to spend on it. As a result, many are still searching for The Platform—that one tool that can address all their needs. Their request for proposal (RFP) documents are veritable kitchen sinks of bells and whistles. They're sure they need a gamified SaaS (software as a service) solution that:

- Recommends content just like Netflix
- Makes content authoring and sharing as easy as TikTok

- Can bend and flex to their always-changing company hierarchy
- Meets all their industry's regulatory requirements
- Connects with every system they already use without any extra IT work
- Has every feature available in offline mode—just in case
- Is able to breach the space/time continuum under 88 miles per hour

Learning technology can do a lot of cool things nowadays, and vendors often promise their solutions can meet all your company's needs. However, if we want to overcome a legacy of technology frustration, we must accept a frank reality: There is no one ring to rule them all (cough cough *Lord of the Rings* reference cough cough).

This isn't just a learning tech thing. It's a fundamental technology principle. Vendors and providers have finite resources and expertise. Their solutions can either do a lot of things OK or a short list of things exceptionally. There's no such thing as a hardware or software tool that will do everything you want in exactly the way you want it—unless you build and maintain it yourself (more on that in a bit).

Let's consider your smartphone again. Imagine you had to force yourself to use one app as a calendar, messenger, inbox, and browser. Sure, you'd only have one button to press, but you'd also be missing out on a ton of functionality provided by specialized apps. The same goes for learning tech. As long as L&D remains focused on finding the "one ring to rule them all," they'll miss out on opportunities to provide even more right-fit digital solutions that meet their workforces' needs.

RedThread Research explained the continuum of workplace learning technology application in the 2019 report *The Art and Science of Designing a Learning Technology Ecosystem*. On one end, an organization relies on a single platform due to limited complexity; low tolerance for risk; focus on top-down, compliance-driven development; and limited budget. On the opposite end, a company leverages a range of tools to support a complex workplace, enable exploration-driven learning, and maximize technology investment (Figure 11-1).

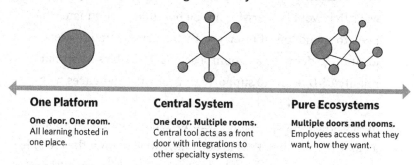

Figure 11-1. Spectrum of Learning Tech Ecosystem Structures

One Platform

One door. One room.
All learning hosted in
one place.

Central System

One door. Multiple rooms.
Central tool acts as a front
door with integrations to
other specialty systems.

Pure Ecosystems

Multiple doors and rooms.
Employees access what they
want, how they want.

Adapted from Johnson and Mehrotra (2019).

The MLE Framework helps you find your spot along this continuum. With its layered approach, the framework aligns learning tactics with the tools needed to facilitate a right-fit experience. It also reinforces two critical observations about L&D tech:

- Any tool that helps people solve problems and improve performance can be classified as a "learning technology," regardless of who manages it.
- Technology-enabled learning is about introducing right-fit digital capabilities, not finding the perfect platform.

In a world where the average organization uses 11 different learning technologies, the MLE Framework provides the structure needed to make the purpose and value of each tool clear and consistent to L&D and its stakeholders.

Before your team starts buying and implementing learning platforms, you must acknowledge and align on the reasons for applying technology to support learning in the first place.

7 Reasons to Apply Learning Tech

Every organization applies technology to enable learning and performance in different ways. Regardless of who owns a technology or which marketplace category it fits within, every learning tool should be evaluated against the same set of foundational criteria:

- **Scale.** Technology helps L&D reach distributed audiences in ways that would otherwise not be possible. It eliminates the need to spend lots of money to fly trainers around to every location to deliver classroom sessions. It enables small-but-mighty L&D teams to support large, diverse audiences with limited resources.
- **Speed.** Technology enables L&D to deploy solutions as soon as they're available. People don't have to wait until they're able to attend a scheduled session to learn something new. Digital solutions also provide an expanded range of methods and modalities that accelerate learning content development and deployment.
- **Consistency.** Technology eliminates the "this is how we really do it here" problem. It makes sure everyone gets the same information, no matter where they work or who their boss is. Digital learning reinforces required job knowledge and behavior when consistency is critical to success.

Scale, speed, and consistency have been driving the proliferation of learning technology since the 1990s. They're the reason companies often opt for e-learning programs over instructor-led training. However, they're just part of the learning tech value proposition. If you're only implementing a tool to gain scale, speed, and consistency, you're missing the mark when it comes to building a right-fit learning digital experience. Modern technology can help us make a much bigger impact through these additional dimensions:

- **Context.** Technology brings learning out of the classroom and into the flow of work. It enables employees to access whatever resources they need in the moment rather than having to wait for a scheduled activity. It also allows L&D to break content apart so it can be consumed iteratively when people have time.
- **Connection.** Technology brings together the people who know and the people who need to know. It transcends physical and temporal barriers to enable people to build expansive knowledge networks on which they can rely to support their performance.

- **Personalization.** Technology can now go beyond scaling the same learning program to a distributed audience. It can also apply data to personalize the learning experience to the individual. L&D can maximize its value proposition by making sure every employee is focused on the development activities that most benefit them and the organization.

- **Equity.** We talked about the opportunity gap in an earlier chapter. The unfortunate reality of workplace learning is that everyone often does not have access to the same opportunities. Employees may be disqualified based on their role, status, location, disability, or other factors. Technology helps close this gap by making development available when, where, and how people can best access it, no matter who they are or what they do.

It's easy to get distracted by cool features and fancy functionality. Who doesn't want to create practice simulations in VR or use an AI assistant to automatically author content? However, to paraphrase noted chaotician Ian Malcolm, just because you can doesn't mean you should.

Keep these seven criteria in mind as you select and apply technology to support learning. Every tool may not check all seven boxes, but your overall tech stack must enable these concepts to maximize the potential of your learning ecosystem.

Designing Persona-Based Digital Learning

The "one ring" approach to digital learning assumes that every employee uses technology the same way. This isn't the case in most organizations. For example, three people may be employed by the same pharmaceutical company. While one works in a heavily credentialed, lab-based scientific role; one works remotely in medical device sales; and one works on the manufacturing line. Their everyday work experiences are different. Their knowledge and skill requirements are different. And their relationships with workplace technology are different. Does this mean they need completely different learning platforms? Maybe . . . and maybe not.

A modern digital learning experience is built a lot like your smartphone. It's constructed with a series of components—chips, sensors, operating system, applications—that blend to shape your user experience. I like my smartphone when the layers function seamlessly. That means I can focus on using the smartphone to solve problems and not worry about how it's constructed. However, when the battery starts to go or the OS chugs when loading an app, I quickly get frustrated and start thinking about getting a new phone. Unfortunately, employees can't opt out of their learning ecosystem (without opting out of their jobs, too). Therefore, L&D must design a digital infrastructure that functions as seamlessly as possible within the day-to-day workflow (Figure 11-2). You must also continue to make upgrades to make sure the infrastructure keeps pace with changing employee needs.

Much like designing a smartphone begins with understanding the user's needs and preferences, building a digital learning experience starts with understanding the needs of your business and persona of your users, incorporating five components: outcomes, experience, data, capability, and digital.

The Outcome Component

What are the biggest priorities related to employee performance within your organization over the next three to five years? Remember, skill requirements are a moving target given the constant pace of business disruption. You may not be able to nail down specific learning goals for the longer term, but beginning the process with a focus on business outcomes will help you avoid the mistake of implementing technology for the sake of implementing technology. If your company plans to open offices in new regions and expand its workforce by 30 percent over the next two years, your tech stack must be ready to enable these outcomes.

The Experience Component

Outline the defining characteristics for each of the employee personas within your audience. Remember, focusing on personas rather than job

Figure 11-2. The Components of a Learning Technology Ecosystem

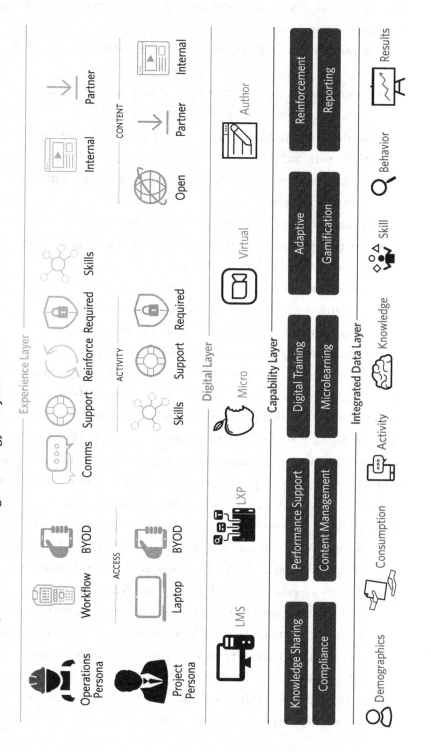

titles or roles allows you to leverage common attributes and reduce the need for additional solutions:

- **Function:** Does this persona work independently or directly with your company's customers and products?
- **Foundation:** Was this persona hired for a specific skill set or are they expected to learn how to do their job?
- **Scale:** Does this persona have a unique role or do they share their workload?
- **Time:** Does this persona have autonomy or is their workload heavily managed?
- **Location:** Where does this persona do their work?
- **Access:** How does this persona access learning and support resources within the workflow?
- **Motivation:** Is this persona focused on meeting foundational job requirements or long-term career goals?
- **Measurement:** Are this persona's performance outcomes determined by subjective or objective measures?

Use these characteristics to design a right-fit experience for the persona. This wireframe represents the various ways tactical support should be experienced within the day-to-day workflow for each employee who fits the persona. Your design is not meant to represent 100 percent of the workplace learning experience. People will always find their own ways to develop their knowledge and skill. Instead, your design should focus on the best ways L&D can provide timely, reliable support on the job. This includes factors such as access, activity, and content:

- **Access:** Which devices will be used most frequently to access digital learning and support resources within the flow of work? There's a good chance mobile devices will play a key role in your digital experience, regardless of audience. Nevertheless, it's important to understand how devices are used on the job so you can align your learning tech stack accordingly. Someone who works in operations may only have access to a handheld scanning device while on the job if they need to search for information. An employee who works in the corporate office likely has more options, such as a company-issued laptop or smartphone, to access digital learning.

- **Activity:** What kinds of learning activities will be most common for this persona? An operations worker in a safety critical environment may have a variety of required training activities, including compliance, core job skills, reinforcement, and ongoing support. A corporate employee who's already a specialist in their role may have some required training but spend most of their formal learning time focused on building new skills as part of ongoing career development.

- **Content:** What types of content will be needed to foster knowledge and skill growth? An operations worker focused on your company's process, products, and services may rely mostly on internal content. A corporate employee looking to develop additional skills may have the time to explore a wider range of content options, including open-source materials from online libraries.

Repeat this process for each persona within your audience to make sure your experience designs align with their workplace contexts. Note any personas with unique experience elements as well as those with over-lapping requirements. This will help you align your technology decisions with clear purpose and value for each persona within your audience.

The Data Component

Now that you know what your end result should look like, it's time to fill out your digital learning experience. Let's start with the foundation: data. You'll need the right data to power your digital learning experience and achieve your organizational goals. Your learning tech must be able to access, capture, apply, and output this data. Therefore, before you select your tools, you must outline your requirements for data input, capture, and output:

- **Data Input:** What data will you need to pull into your learning experience to power your design? For example, you will likely need to access people data, such as employee records, to provision users within your digital systems and target training accordingly. You may also require operational data, including business KPIs, to determine the impact of your learning programs and adjust your strategies. Identify the types of data available outside the learning tech stack, how it is stored, and if or how it can be accessed to enable right-fit learning experiences.

- **Data Capture:** What data will you need to capture within your digital learning experience to power your design? Most LMS platforms collect basic learning data, including course completions, test scores, and survey results. Will this be enough, or will you need additional metrics, such as user feedback, knowledge growth, or search results? Make a list of the data points that must be captured within the learning experience to optimize the experience for each employee.

- **Data Output:** What data will you need to push out of your learning experience to power your design? This may include familiar requirements, such as learning data exports, visualizations, and reporting. You should also explore advanced learning data practices, such as sharing skills data with workforce management tools to inform scheduling, talent acquisition, and mobility functions.

This data conversation should not happen within an L&D silo. Collaborate with internal and external partners to clarify your data requirements and capabilities as you construct the digital experience. We'll dive into the connection between the MLE Framework and measurement practices in more detail in the next chapter.

The Capability Component

Next, you must figure out how to bring your persona-based learning experience to life through technology. In a traditional procurement process, this means filling out a lengthy RFP spreadsheet with a laundry list of feature requirements. Some organizations try to accelerate this process by using an RFP template from an external consultant that already includes every must-have learning tech feature available. This is a mistake. There are no "must-have learning tech features." Taking a feature-focused approach to learning technology gives vendors control of the process. L&D ends up making decisions based on a vendor's ability to check as many boxes as possible (and they're all very good at box checking, no matter what their solutions actually do). Instead, look for tools that can bring your experience design to life in the simplest and most impactful ways possible.

Use the MLE Framework as a guide when identifying the capabilities you must provide within your digital learning experience. You may be thinking, "What's the difference between a feature and a capability?" A digital capability is the connection point between technology and experience. It explains what people must be able to do within your digital learning ecosystem. However, it does not define exactly how they should do it.

Let's take the shared knowledge layer of the MLE Framework as an example. While designing your persona-based experience for a corporate audience, you determine that you need to offer employees the opportunity to share proven practices with their peers. Therefore, you include "crowdsource proven practices" as a required capability. If you were taking a feature-focused approach to your technology selection process, you may instead create a list of features like:

- Record video and upload from any device
- Edit video and upload with description and tags
- Approve, decline, and resubmit videos via approval workflow
- Curate and create video playlists
- Search for video using metadata and an audio transcript

This list predetermines how technology must function before you've explored your real-life options. It pushes providers to find ways to check every box instead of collaborating to find the best way to solve your problem using their tools. Sure, you may ultimately discover that many of these features are important in executing your "crowdsource proven practices" capability. However, by focusing on what people need to do—not how they should do it—you open the door to a wider range of potential right-fit digital solutions.

Start by listing the capabilities required to activate each layer within the MLE Framework for each persona within your audience. For example, the performance support layer may include "submit questions to SMEs" while reinforcement may include "simulate customer interactions." In addition to the MLE Framework layers, include capability items for your user experience and data functions. For example, you may list accessibility standards or mobile access within user experience. Data may include compliance reporting requirements and single sign-on (SSO) integration.

Once you've outlined your full capability list, review it from the user's perspective. Can you realistically expect employees to leverage these capabilities as part of their ongoing learning and support experience? Ask stakeholders, SMEs, and employees to share their thoughts as well. Once your capability list is firmly grounded in reality, it's (finally) time to make technology decisions.

The Digital Component

Which tool(s) will provide employees with the capabilities needed to develop their skills and improve their performance? Notice my effective use of the (s) when I referred to the tool(s) you'll select. If you support 40 people who all do the same kind of work within the same context, you may find a single technology that can execute your full capabilities list and enable a right-fit digital learning experience. However, if you support 40,000 people across multiple business units, geographies, and personas, you're going to need that (s).

I've never heard of an L&D team with an unlimited budget. Even companies on the Fortune 100 are looking for ways to consolidate their learning tech stacks. The goal may not be to find the one tool that does everything, but you should still look to limit your technology spend. This includes everything from software licenses and hardware maintenance to administrative headcount and IT support needs. Therefore, the first place you should look for technology that can fulfill as many of your capability requirements as possible is inside your own four walls.

Share your experience designs and capability lists with internal technology partners. This includes operations, communications, marketing, and—of course—IT. Identify tools that may fit your needs that are already in use within the organization. Remember, it doesn't have to be called learning technology to play a part within your learning ecosystem. Ask for permission to experiment with available tools to prove their value in application. If something catches on and proves to be of value, collaborate with your partners to expand its use. In the shared knowledge chapter, I told the story of how I discovered the wiki platform Confluence within my contact center operation. If I hadn't collaborated with marketing and IT to close my shared knowledge capability gaps, I would have had to spend a lot more time and money looking for a solution.

Once you've exhausted your internal technology options, it's time to go shopping. Start by clarifying your budget requirements, timelines, and resources. There's no point in exploring tools that you can't afford or don't have the capacity to administer.

Collaborate with internal and external peers to identify potential solutions that meet your needs. Instead of asking people "Which LXP platforms should I look at," stay focused on your experience design and be open to exploring new and unfamiliar options.

Ditch the standard RFP spreadsheet when you start meeting with providers. Instead, share your experience design (Figure 11-2). Challenge providers to demonstrate how their technology can help execute your design while staying within your budget, timeline, and resource limits. Involve your IT, HR, and operational partners to make sure all potential tools meet organizational requirements, including data security, privacy, bandwidth, integrations, and devices.

Stacking the Layers of Your Digital Learning Ecosystem

Here's how you design a persona-based digital learning ecosystem:

1. Always start with outcomes—the learning and performance problems people will be expected to solve using your digital ecosystem.
2. Design right-fit learning experiences for each persona within your audience, including considerations for how digital

learning will be accessed, the types of activities in which people will need to engage, and the variety of content to be used within the experience.

3. Identify your data requirements, including data that must be pulled into the ecosystem, captured within it, and shared outside it.

4. List the necessary digital capabilities (not features) to bring your learning experience designs to life for each persona.

5. Select technology with the proven ability to execute your required capabilities in the simplest, most impactful ways possible.

Each digital learning ecosystem is unique. Some use a small selection of tools—perhaps just a light LMS and a rapid authoring tool—due to their limited capability requirements and simple experience designs. Others apply a lengthy list of solutions—such as LMS, LXP, authoring tools, virtual reality simulations, microlearning platforms, online classrooms—to meet diverse employee needs within complex organizations. In every case, L&D must make smart decisions that reduce the white space within their technology stacks, maximize return on investment, and provide right-fit support for every employee.

That's a quick summary of how modern L&D teams select technology. Implementing technology is an entirely different story—one that I don't have enough words left to explore in this book. Instead, check out Donald Taylor's *Learning Technologies in the Workplace: How to Successfully Implement Learning Technologies in Organizations*. After all, Jane Hart said "So much of modern workplace learning relies on technologies and yet nobody has written a definitive guide to their implementation—until now. It's readable, insightful and useful and I recommend it." Sounds awesome, right? Tell Don that JD sent you!

Before we move on, let's explore a few additional considerations you should keep in mind when making informed technology decisions: build versus buy, integration, and measurement.

Should You Build or Buy Learning Tech?

You're not going to find a tool that does things exactly the way you want, even in a crowded technology marketplace. So that raises the question, should you just build your own tool? This debate has been raging for as long as learning tech has existed. It's just taken on different forms over time.

Technology went into the cloud in the mid-2000s, prompting an ongoing conversation within enterprise IT about whether it was better to host software using your own hardware infrastructure or by renting someone else's. Amazon Web Services (AWS), Google Cloud Platform (GCP), and Microsoft Azure made it cheaper and more efficient to go off-premises without fear of downtimes or security breaches. As a result, 87 percent of LMS users were in the cloud by 2015 (Pappas 2021).

Software then evolved from being just stored in the cloud to being operated up there too. Software as a service (SaaS) took advantage of increased broadband access, growing use of web-based interfaces, and standardized web technology to create the licensing and delivery models we know today. In 2010, SaaS accounted for just 6 percent of enterprise software revenue (Roche, Schneider, and Shah 2021). By 2018, that number had grown to 29 percent, or $150 billion globally. Of course, this varies by industry due to considerations such as data security and functionality requirements. For example, in 2018 only 21 percent of government applications were SaaS as compared to 38 percent in professional services.

SaaS dominates the learning technology space today. From LXPs to authoring software, most of the tools used to support digital learning in the workplace exist in the cloud. This has shifted the debate from "cloud vs. on-premises" to "buy vs. build." Hundreds of vendors around the world offer SaaS subscription models and platform customizations so L&D can have immediate access to technology. At the same time, open-source platforms, no-code tools, and third-party developers give L&D the option to build the exact technology they need.

So, should you buy or build the systems needed to bring your right-fit digital learning experience to life?

The answer is yet another unsatisfying "it depends." A build strategy that works for a global enterprise with 400,000 employees may not work for a medium-sized business with 2,000 people. Rather than rely on hard and fast rules, L&D must weigh the pros and cons when deciding whether to buy or build technology (Table 11-1).

Table 11-1. Pros and Cons of Buying Tech

Pros	Cons
• **Proven capability and scale:** L&D can see and touch the tech before implementation through pilots and demos. They can also leverage case studies and referrals to attest to the capability of the tech at scale. • **Limited maintenance:** The tech provider is responsible for handling ongoing bug fixes, upgrades, and support tickets. • **Experienced guidance:** The provider has implemented the tech before, likely for similar organizations. They can bring this experience to bear during your implementation. • **Persistent innovation:** Providers must continuously innovate their products to remain competitive. L&D reaps the benefits of this through new features and services.	• **Limited customization:** The provider may offer basic tech customizations, such as company branding and opting in or out of select features. However, the base product is the base product, regardless of how you use it. • **Ongoing subscription fees:** SaaS solutions charge monthly or annual fees for seat licenses or activity. In many cases, you must pay for the tech whether it gets used or not. This puts pressure on L&D to maximize engagement to improve ROI. • **Vendor reliance:** The more a platform is used, the more reliant L&D may become on the provider to execute their strategy. This may become problematic if the provider is unreliable.

Of course, many of the pros and cons for building technology are the inverse of buying it (Table 11-2).

Admittedly, there are a lot more cons to building your own learning tech than pros. However, if you really need technical capability that does not already exist and you have the development resources to make it work, it can be a viable option. Otherwise, there are so many powerful and unique tools available in the marketplace, it almost always makes sense to start by exploring what providers have to offer.

Table 11-2. Pros and Cons of Building Tech

Pros	Cons
• **Custom functionality:** L&D can build whatever solution it wants. The sky's the limit—as long as they have the development resources to make it happen. • **Up-front costs:** The cost to build custom tech is heavily front loaded due to software and infrastructure development. Once the system is in place, ongoing costs are limited to maintenance, enhancement, and service fees. • **Freedom to adapt:** L&D can update their custom solution whenever they want to meet changing business demands. They don't have to wait for a provider to include a new feature on a future road map.	• **Product vision:** L&D must be able to outline a clear vision for the product and how it will be developed. If you don't have product development experience in a technology setting, this may be a complicated and lengthy process. • **Unproven capability and scale:** No one has ever seen or used your custom solution before. You don't know if it will work as intended until you make the investment to build and test it. • **Ongoing maintenance:** L&D is responsible for all ongoing maintenance work, including bug fixes, browser compatibility, and upgrades. This may be completed in-house or outsourced depending on your available resources. • **Lack of guidance:** L&D is on their own when building a custom solution. You may hire a consultant to provide high-level guidance, but it's ultimately up to you to make product design decisions. • **Limited innovation:** sThe solution will remain at version 1 until you make the decision to invest and upgrade. L&D has limited resources already without the need to maintain an innovation road map for their homegrown technology.

Rethinking Integration

Integration is one of the buzziest words in workplace technology for a good reason. If you must deploy a growing number of tools to help people do their jobs, it makes sense that you'd want those tools to function together as seamlessly as possible. On paper, this should simplify the technology experience for both users and administrators. The challenge is that the word integration can mean a lot of different things, especially when it comes to learning technology. For example, integration may refer to the desire to:

- Share credentialing information between systems as part of single sign-on
- Provision users into a system via an automated spreadsheet upload
- Push course completion and test score data to a system of record via an application programming interface (API)
- Add learning functionality to another application via a software development kit (SDK)
- Apply out-of-the-box connectors to aggregate content from multiple subscription services
- Use deep links to access content hosted in a content management system (CMS) from the LMS

This is another reason why beginning your technology journey with a persona-based ecosystem design is so crucial. The purposeful blend of experience, data, capabilities, and digital tools will clarify your integration needs. While some systems are built to function together seamlessly, the fact of the matter is that we don't live or work in a perfectly integrated technological world. Every organization administers systems and handles data in different ways. Technology providers try to apply consistent standards to make integrations as simple as possible, but they're unable to account for the needs and preferences of every company. Add to that a pile of regulatory requirements that vary by region, and integrations become a lot harder than just checking a box on an RFP.

The MLE Framework helps L&D apply a range of tools to foster a right-fit, continuous learning and support experience. To fit learning within the everyday workflow, the experience must be frictionless, embedded, and purposeful. At the same time, L&D often has limited technology resources to build and maintain technical integrations. IT may be able to help, but their customer-facing projects will always take priority. Therefore, L&D must approach the concept of integration from two perspectives: strategic and technical (Figure 11-3).

Figure 11-3. L&D Integration Points

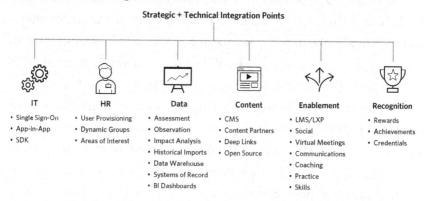

Strategic Integration

Just because two systems aren't connected doesn't mean they can't work together (wow . . . a triple negative!). Every tool within the learning technology ecosystem must be strategically integrated. This means each system has a clearly defined purpose that is understood by everyone within the audience. Employees know why they should use the tool within the workflow. Subject matter experts and stakeholders know how they should leverage the tool to support their projects. L&D maintains this purpose to simplify the user experience.

Consider a learning tech stack that includes an LMS and a SharePoint site. Both systems can store documents and host online discussions. However, if these capabilities are applied differently by project, users will struggle to understand where to go for different parts of their learning and support experience. Therefore, L&D must clarify the purpose for each system. In this case, formal online training may be completed in the LMS while shared knowledge and performance support activities take place on SharePoint because it's closer to the workflow. If a stake-holder asks L&D to upload documents to the LMS, L&D must push back and suggest the information be added to SharePoint to maintain each tool's purpose. L&D may also add links within each system to help users navigate between tools to find related materials.

Technical Integration

Systems should only be integrated via API or other technical means when it adds clear value. SSO and user provisioning are two clear-cut examples, as they simplify the user experience and reduce administrative burden. L&D must be ready to set up and maintain these technical integrations in collaboration with providers and IT partners. Think twice about integrations that may create unnecessary disruption. For example, if a vendor does not provide significant notice and documentation for major system updates, you may not want to risk breaking the entire ecosystem due to a sudden lack of compatibility with one tool. This is especially important when learning technologies integrate with other business-critical systems, such as security, sales, or workforce management platforms.

Consider a learning tech stack that includes an LMS and an adaptive learning platform. The LMS is the validated system of record, meaning all employee learning data must be housed there for regulatory purposes. The LMS also hosts all proprietary learning materials. The adaptive learning platform delivers microlearning and reinforcement training to frontline workers. The organization implements this tool in addition to the LMS used by corporate team members because its personalized, mobile-first experience better meets the needs of their deskless employees. L&D doesn't have the capacity to manage the same content across both systems, so they work with the two providers to integrate their platforms. Digital content is stored in the LMS and appears within employees' adaptive learning sessions via API. Data from these online sessions is pushed to the LMS to maintain a single system of record. Furthermore, both platforms integrate with the company's HR system for provisioning and authentication.

Measuring the Value of Tech

There's an entire chapter on data coming up next, but we can't finish our technology discussion without exploring how you can assess the value of your digital tools.

Workplace technology has traditionally been viewed as a capital expenditure (CAPEX). Buying software was an expense a business incurred for future benefit. Therefore, management accounted for technology in the same way as buying a new building. However, the proliferation of SaaS technology has shifted this perspective. Today, companies don't own learning tech. They rent it by the month or year. When their contract is up, they must either renew or move to a new provider to maintain the same kind of capability. While implementation projects are budgeted as CAPEX due to their considerable upfront costs, learning technology is now an operational expense (OPEX). This puts added pressure on L&D to justify its digital value, especially as businesses continuously look to reduce costs.

L&D measurement tends to focus on content, not systems. Some tools, such as sales enablement platforms, are implemented to solve specific problems and therefore have value that is easier to quantify. However, most learning platforms have become part of the standard workflow. They exist to solve a variety of problems, from compliance and sales to company culture and product knowledge. This makes learning tech more vulnerable to cost cutting measures, because its value is not directly connected to revenue-generating activities. This also makes it more difficult for L&D to gain buy-in for additional technology investment.

I don't have an exact formula for measuring the value of learning technology. But I do have a short list of factors you should consider as you refine your digital road map:

- **Engagement.** Are people using the tool with the intended frequency? Employees don't have to log into a system every day to gain value. However, if most people are not using it with any regularity, what's the point of paying for it?

- **Impact.** Does the tool play a critical role in enabling performance improvement? The platform itself may not be as directly responsible for knowledge and skill development as the activities and content it delivers, but could you provide the same type of employee support without the technology?
- **Sentiment.** Do people like to use the tool as part of their workflow? Features and functions don't matter if people get frustrated when trying to use a technology because it's too complicated or unreliable.
- **Agility.** Does the tool strengthen your overall ecosystem? Technology should not be solely assessed on its own. Rather, you must look at the entire technology stack to make sure you consider how tools support and enable one another.
- **Education.** Does the tool improve your overall team capability? All technology comes with a learning curve. The best providers share insights gathered from working with an array of organizations to educate their customers and advance their practices. The value of this collaboration must be considered alongside the technology itself.
- **Innovation.** Does the tool propel your strategy forward? Smart technology providers invest heavily in research and development (R&D) to remain competitive in a crowded marketplace. This effort provides an ongoing stream of new digital capabilities that may otherwise not be available to your organization.

You should assess the value of your digital ecosystem—including tools you apply but do not administer—on an annual basis. Compare the value these tools provide against the total cost of ownership, including license fees, administrative capacity, staff training, and IT support. This recurring assessment will help you determine if and when changes are necessary to maintain the ROI of your technology stack.

The Not-So-Distant Future of Learning Tech

I started this chapter by saying "technology is now the face of L&D." But this evolution isn't just about learning. Work has become a digital experience. Desked employees collaborate through Zoom sessions, Slack messages, and shared documents. Deskless workers use handheld devices to manage workflows, engage with customers, and access timely resources. The pandemic accelerated the digital transformation of work out of necessity, opening the door to new remote and hybrid work models. As a result, L&D followed suit and accelerated its own use of technology. However, the increased use of tech in learning and development does not necessarily equate to true digital transformation.

The internet transformed the way people accessed and shared information in the late 1990s and early 2000s. In grade school, I had to get my parents to drive me to the library so I could find the information I needed to write a report. In high school, I had to endure the hideous dial-up connection sound when I opened AOL to surf the web. In college, it was all Google all the time. By the time I entered the workforce, we all had Blackberrys, and the iPhone was on the horizon. Over the course of 10 years, technology changed the way I engaged with the world.

What happened in L&D over that same period? Instructor-led courses became e-learning modules. That's about it. Sure, L&D benefitted from the additional scale, speed, and consistency that computer-based training enabled. But the same technology that transformed everyday life did not fundamentally shift the way organizations approached workplace learning. This trend continued through another decade of digital evolution as social and mobile technology became the standard. Burdened by operational demands and limited resources, L&D was unable to align the workplace learning experience with people's everyday digital reality.

Today, L&D finds itself at another critical pivot point because of disruption. Technology is once again changing the way we live our lives, in everything from how we shop to how we date. Will L&D rethink the ways organizations can leverage technology to help people solve problems, develop skills, and improve performance? Or will we again graft a traditional mindset onto the next generation of digital tools? According to 2021 research by Brandon Hall Group, most organizations plan to increase their investment in digital learning moving forward. At the top of the list were:

- Virtual synchronous classrooms (77 percent)
- Microlearning (71 percent)
- E-learning modules (71 percent)

Only 31 percent of organizations are making moderate to heavy investments in artificial intelligence (AI) and machine learning. Just 19 percent are ramping up applications of virtual and augmented reality. L&D may be using more technology more often, but our mindset regarding how technology can help people improve their performance has yet to evolve.

As we create the next future of work, L&D must rethink the way we use technology to achieve organizational goals. This will require considerable investment in our own R&D efforts. We must dedicate capacity to exploring and experimenting with new tools and frameworks. We must partner with technology providers to inform their ongoing road map development and understand how concepts like AI are fundamentally changing the way technology works. We must dig into buzzy topics like the metaverse and determine if and how these digital capabilities may be applied to solve familiar problems in new ways. L&D must foster a technology-enabled mindset so organizations can graduate beyond the basics of computer-based training and reap the full benefits of digital learning, including context, connection, personalization, and equity.

The MLE Framework helps L&D teams expand their digital perspective by applying right-fit technology to foster continuous learning. It makes solving problems at work feel more like solving problems in everyday life. It helps L&D translate everyday digital tools into workplace applications. Rather than assume employees will engage on Yammer because it looks and feels like Facebook, the MLE Framework shifts the focus from functionality to behavior and makes learning at work feel as simple and frictionless as using the apps on your smartphone.

Chapter 12

The Data Side of the Story

Power Your Learning System With
Continuous Measurement

SPOILER
ALERT

It's time to talk about measurement, the biggest challenge facing L&D today. We're
going to cover some basic tips for improving data practices, including:
- The four reasons L&D needs to invest in measurement
- What L&D can learn about data from marketing
- How to find and access the right data
- How to shift from programmatic to continuous measurement

L&D has a measurement problem. Of course, I'm not talking about your
team (wink wink). I'm talking about all those other L&D teams trying to
figure out how to move beyond butts in seats as an indicator of organizational impact.

Measurement is the biggest capability gap in the L&D profession.
According to Brandon Hall's *2019 Learning Strategy Survey,* 69 percent of
companies say the inability to measure learning's impact represents a
challenge to achieving critical learning outcomes. This data fluency gap
extends beyond L&D and throughout the HR function. Just 23 percent
of HR professionals are comfortable using analytics without guidance,
according to research from Insight222.

The good news is that most L&D teams know they have a data problem. How many times have you heard a peer bemoan the inability to get
past Level 2 of The Kirkpatrick Model (Figure 12-1)?

Figure 12-1. The Kirkpatrick Model vs. Reality

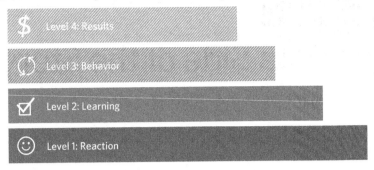

And how many alternative frameworks have been introduced to address this issue over the past 50 years? Kaufman. Anderson. Brinkerhoff. Van Pelt. Phillips. Thalheimer. L&D has so many measurement and evaluation frameworks from which to choose that you probably aren't even sure which of those names I made up.

The bad news is that, despite all the models, frameworks, sessions, articles, and webinars, L&D still struggles with data. Can we solve this decades-old problem by the end of this chapter? Absolutely not. Instead, I hope the MLE Framework helps you shift your organization's perspective on the relationship between learning and data so we can finally begin to fix L&D measurement.

4 Reasons to Solve the Data Problem

Measurement isn't going to fix itself. It's going to require strategic effort from L&D and its partners. Unfortunately, your team already has a lot going on, and measurement strategy may not seem like an item to address ASAP compared with timely operational demands and regulatory requirements. This is why, according to the Corporate Research Forum (2021), 69 percent of organizations with more than 10,000 employees have entire teams devoted to people analytics.

Becoming data-enabled requires investment. This may sound daunting if your L&D function is already doing its best to get by with limited resources. However, improving your data practices is well worth the time, capacity, and effort required, especially if you hope to grow the L&D function over the long term.

If you firmly believe L&D needs to get better with data but constantly get pushback from your peers, managers, or partners, here are four justifications you can use to influence their perspective.

1. Good Measurement Makes L&D Proactive

How does L&D know when a solution is needed?

L&D is a reactive business function. We wait for stakeholders to request our help as a shared service. Our limited capacity is prioritized based on the next big initiative, such as a new product release or regulatory change. This may or may not have anything to do with the challenges employees face on the job every day. If L&D does act based on a timely performance issue, we usually don't get involved until after the problem has negatively impacted the organization.

L&D must become proactive to deliver the most possible value to the business. You can't wait for people to get hurt (literally and metaphorically) before you offer up right-fit solutions. Instead, L&D must leverage data to identify prevailing performance trends and proactively step in to help people who are struggling. But, to take this step forward with our measurement practices, you need more than learning data. L&D must recognize that learning data is part of the greater business data puzzle. You still need to know how learning solutions are being leveraged, but you must also connect these initiatives to on-the-job results.

2. Good Measurement Validates Impact

What's the point of doing something if you don't know if it works?

My favorite smile sheet question of all time is "Do you intend to use what you've learned on the job?" It embodies everything that's wrong with learning measurement. Intent does not matter, especially during a training event. Results matter. Good or bad, they often occur well after training is completed.

Every company function is expected to deliver measurable results. Why should L&D be held to a different standard than sales, marketing, or product management? L&D must connect the dots between learning solutions and performance outcomes. Otherwise, you'll always have a hard time justifying added investment in skill development. Executives don't care how many hours of training were delivered per employee last year. They need validation that their L&D investments are fostering a capable workforce and value-added job performance.

3. Good Measurement Unlocks the Future

How can you apply advanced practices without advanced data?

Imagine a future in which you can provide personalized support for every employee, regardless of the size of your audience or L&D team. Employees receive automated coaching and content recommendations via chat based on their current knowledge and skill gaps. When they log into your learning platform, the experience adapts to their personal needs and preferences. As they grow their skills, employees are automatically matched with open projects and positions. L&D can track the impact of their learning solutions in real time and make proactive adjustments to maximize their business value.

This isn't the future. All these capabilities exist right now thanks in large part to artificial intelligence (AI) and robotic process automation (RPA). However, you can't offer this version of a workplace learning experience without the data needed to power the technology. As long as your L&D function struggles with measurement, you'll set an artificial limit on how far you can advance your practices.

4. Good Measurement Is Critical to the Skills Economy

How do you know which skills your organization does or doesn't possess?

Skill is now considered the fundamental unit of the employee experience. Every role can be broken down into its foundational skill requirements. Skills are the reason people get hired, trained, and assigned. They are the key enabler of performance and therefore have become the true currency of the workplace. Unfortunately, the skills economy crashes when you can't figure out which skills people do or don't have across your organization.

Traditional L&D measurement models focus on timely knowledge acquisition, not sustained performance capability. Skills take time to develop. They degrade when not maintained. They can only be validated through real-world application. Therefore, to adopt a skills-based approach, L&D must first improve its measurement strategy. Otherwise, you won't be able to keep up with the evolving skills needs of your business.

Why L&D Measurement Really Fails

Traditional learning measurement tries to shove a square peg into a round hole. It doesn't matter which model to which you subscribe. The issue runs much deeper. This is why so many different reasons were cited by L&D professionals when Brandon Hall Group asked about their lack of measurement capability:

- We don't have time or staff (47 percent)
- We don't have proper metrics (41 percent)
- We don't have the technology to support it (39 percent)
- It's too difficult to link learning to outcomes (33 percent)
- It's too difficult to assess (29 percent)
- We don't see a need (4 percent)

I've run into every one of these measurement challenges during my career. My L&D teams were often only lucky enough to get management buy in to deliver the training program. Asking for support to conduct additional measurement felt like a fairytale. In some cases, stakeholders had the data we needed but were unwilling to share it with us. They didn't see the need or trust us to properly handle their sensitive data when the only metrics we had shared in the past were benign items like course completions and test scores.

L&D has struggled with data because our overall approach to learning does not match the realities of modern workplace performance. There's only so much data you can gather during a structured training program that takes place during a limited period of time. You can track who completed the course, which parts of the content they touched, and how they felt about the experience. You may be able to track knowledge change using pre- and post-assessment, but that doesn't mean knowledge is retained or applied during the days, weeks, and months after training. Learning isn't constant. It ebbs and flows over time based on a variety of factors (Figure 12-2).

Figure 12-2. How People Think Learning Works vs. How It Really Works

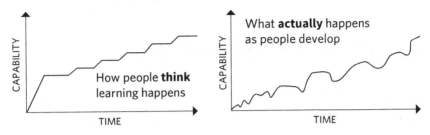

L&D's programmatic infrastructure inherently limits our measurement capability. Our decades-old models made sense when training primarily took place in classrooms and skill requirements were more stable. Today, they simply don't generate the data needed to keep pace with changing workplace needs. Going beyond basic metrics to reach Levels 3 and 4 of the Kirkpatrick Model requires time and resources L&D simply doesn't have.

A Lesson From Marketing

L&D can learn a lot from our friends in marketing, including how to build engaging content and how to design a campaign that facilitates behavior change. However, the best lesson we can take from our friends down the metaphorical hall is how to become a data-enabled function. After all, marketers track more than your ad consumption. They use everything they can learn about you to serve up targeted advertising and influence your buying decisions. Marketing knows how to measure impact, but this wasn't always the case.

Marketing professionals found themselves in a similar spot to L&D in the 1990s and early 2000s. Before the internet became ubiquitous, marketers leaned on traditional tactics, such as direct mail, print ads, and radio and television spots. Oh . . . and billboards. Marketers applied a limited understanding of their audience to attract as many eyes to their content as possible. Then, they did their best to correlate changes in business results to marketing activities. Could they confirm that driving past a billboard caused you to purchase a new breakfast cereal? No. They just knew sales increased in the region after the billboards went up. Correlation is not causation, but it's the best they could do with the tools they had.

Fast forward 20 years and marketing is the most data-enabled function within most businesses. Rather than be bound by the limits of antiquated tactics, marketing innovated their practices alongside technology. The internet led to the rise of digital marketing. Mobile and social technology provided even more access to quality data. Sure, marketers still use billboards, but they're now a small piece of a strategic toolset.

It's time for L&D to catch up with marketing by expanding our ecosystem to include more data-rich tactics. The MLE Framework will not solve all your measurement problems, but it will challenge you to rethink your data practices. As you shift away from implementing courses as your default learning solution, you'll no longer be able to rely on antiquated metrics like the average number of training hours per employee to validate L&D impact. Instead, you must leverage the MLE Framework to tell a more holistic story through the collection, analysis, and application of a wider range of learning and performance metrics.

The Principles of Good Data

L&D needs more data, but you also need the right data. You need data that helps you understand the needs of your employees and how their performance does (or does not) change as a result of learning solutions.

As you begin to identify the metrics that really matter within your ecosystem and how you will capture them, consider the five principles of good data:

- **Volume:** The appropriate amount of data must be collected to make meaningful observations and identify persistent trends.
- **Velocity:** Data must be gathered and analyzed at the speed required to inform decision making.
- **Variety:** Different types of data are needed to paint a holistic picture.

- **Veracity:** Data must be trustworthy and free of bias and disruptive outliers.
- **Value:** Data must be selected for inclusion based on its proven importance.

L&D must build a robust data infrastructure based on these five principles to overcome historic measurement gaps and power a robust learning and performance ecosystem.

Finding the Right Data

Figuring out where to start is often the biggest obstacle when it comes to fixing L&D measurement. Like everything else we've discussed in this book, it will take time to evolve your data practices. You may have a grand vision for how data should inform your modern learning strategy, but you'll likely have to implement it piece by piece while continuing to deal with timely stakeholder requests.

Improving measurement begins with identifying the types of data you'll need to power your learning ecosystem. Specific metrics will vary by organization and use case. That said, most high-value data fits within four categories: operational, people, performance, and learning.

Operational Data

How do you know there's a performance problem in the first place?

Start by exploring the same operational data stakeholders use to measure performance. This may include sales revenue, basket size, and net promoter scores in a retail environment, or first-call resolution, average hold time, and quality scores in a contact center. This data is essential to validating the impact of L&D solutions. If stakeholders are unable (or unwilling) to share, your measurement capabilities will be limited as a result.

Operational data is sometimes referred to as business data by L&D professionals. This is a misnomer that unnecessarily separates the data collected and applied by L&D from that used by the rest of the organization. Learning data should be viewed as a subset of business data instead of an entirely different category.

People Data

Who is L&D trying to help solve this problem?

This is the easiest data for L&D to access. Organizations have lots of employee data. This includes demographics, roles, team structures, locations, tenure, and more. You probably already partner with HR to use this data to provision LMS users and assign training content. Expanding your use of people data will help you better understand your audience and target solutions to the right individuals and groups.

Performance Data

What is happening on the job?

Behavioral data is typically included in L&D measurement models as an indicator of real-world knowledge transfer. However, it's typically collected outside L&D and therefore requires support from operational partners. As a result, it's hard to access and even harder to collect consistently. Some operations have built-in mechanisms for capturing behavior data. For example, safety-critical environments such as warehouses and manufacturing facilities employ auditors to record performance data and mitigate business risk.

Learning Data

How are employee knowledge and skill changing?

Learning data is limited by L&D tactics. If you rely primarily on SCORM-based courses, you're likely tracking metrics such as seat times, completions, test scores, and survey feedback. More advanced data standards, such as the Experience API (xAPI), help L&D collect more detailed user data, including how people engage with learning activities. The MLE Framework enables you to expand the concept of learning data beyond structured training activities. Each framework layer includes a range of potential data points. Here are a few examples by layer:

- **Shared knowledge.** Intranet sites and wikis provide metrics similar to modern websites. This includes visits, unique visitors, pageviews, shares, time spent, locations, devices, and search terms.

- **Performance support.** Chat tools and social platforms offer metrics such as engagement volume, popular days and times, popular topics, and user sentiment.
- **Reinforcement.** Simulations and scenario-based questions allow you to track changes in knowledge and skill over time through application in risk-free environments.
- **Coaching.** Coaching support tools allow you to track engagement, on-the-job behavior, and employee feedback.
- **Pull training.** On-demand learning platforms help you understand areas of interest beyond required training, including search results, content consumption, content ratings, and content shares.
- **Push training.** Whether it's online or on-the-job, required training allows you to track employee progress, completion, immediate knowledge and skill changes, and participant feedback.

This is far from a comprehensive list of L&D data requirements, but hopefully you see how applying data from different categories will help you proactively determine the need for and impact of L&D solutions.

Shift to Continuous Measurement

The MLE Framework establishes consistent channels through which L&D can rapidly deliver right-fit learning and support solutions. This concept also applies to measurement. The tactics within each layer provide continuous data collection and application opportunities (Figure 12-3). This transforms measurement into a repeatable, scalable process. Rather than building measurement tactics into every training program, L&D can leverage the same tactics over and over again, regardless of the topic or solution.

Figure 12-3. Continuous Application and Measurement Cycle

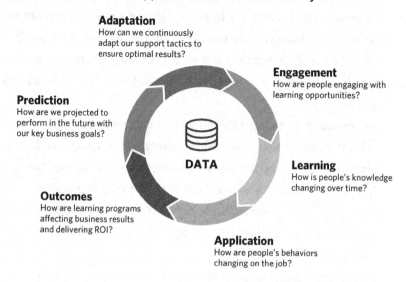

Adaptation
How can we continuously adapt our support tactics to ensure optimal results?

Engagement
How are people engaging with learning opportunities?

Prediction
How are we projected to perform in the future with our key business goals?

DATA

Learning
How is people's knowledge changing over time?

Outcomes
How are learning programs affecting business results and delivering ROI?

Application
How are people's behaviors changing on the job?

The MLE Framework's approach to continuous learning measurement is grounded in L&D's understanding of business priorities and employee personas. While specific metrics and tactics vary by organization, this approach helps L&D capture a critical set of insights:

- **Engagement.** How are people engaging with learning and support resources?
- **Learning.** How is people's knowledge changing over time?
- **Application.** How are people's behaviors changing on the job?
- **Outcomes.** How are business results and performance outcomes changing?

When captured continuously, these insights will help you connect the dots and measure the impact of learning solutions on business results. You can also apply advanced analytical tools, such as machine learning models, to this data to identify trends and proactively adjust your solutions:

- **Prediction.** Is the organization projected to achieve key business goals based on current performance trends?
- **Adaptation.** How can L&D modify its strategy to ensure optimal results?

A continuous measurement approach helps L&D leverage data to ask better questions and proactively improve solutions rather than waiting until a training program concludes to find out that it missed the mark.

As you shift from programmatic to continuous measurement and apply data in new ways, you must also keep a few guiding principles in mind:

- **Governance.** Data must be collected, analyzed, and applied ethically, responsibly, and transparently. Employees should always have the opportunity to question how data is used to inform their workplace experience. Measurement practices must align with company, industry, and regional standards, such as the General Data Protection Regulation (GDPR) within the European Union.
- **Sentiment.** L&D professionals spend a lot of time poking fun at Level 1 evaluations (smile sheets). Survey data may not be as important as behavior observations or business outcomes, but employee sentiment is an important part of a learning ecosystem. L&D must stay connected with its audience and ensure they feel properly supported, even when other metrics point toward positive results.
- **Interoperability.** L&D must be able to pull and push data to and from operational systems to power its solutions. For example, L&D must capture skills data so that it can be shared to operations systems such as workforce management and project assignment tools. Therefore, L&D must work with data and technology partners to ensure data interoperability.
- **Reporting.** Any L&D measurement approach must check certain boxes. If a regulator requires seat time to be tracked within compliance programs, L&D must ensure this data is collected and reported—even if it's not perceived to be particularly valuable. All reports should be actionable, not just descriptive, so managers and administrators can leverage L&D insights to make timely, reliable decisions.

The First Step Toward Improved Measurement

That's how you fit a square peg into a round hole. You totally change the shape of the peg (learning measurement) so that it seamlessly fits within the hole (workplace reality). We've only scratched the surface of data strategy in this chapter, and it probably sounds like a lot of work already. If L&D wants to keep pace with organizational needs, deliver clear business value, and advance our practices along the way, we must fix our data problem.

Thankfully, you don't have to figure this out all on your own. Chances are the smartest data people within your organization don't work in L&D. If you work in a big company with lots of resources, you may be able to hire data specialists to improve your measurement practices as their full-time job. However, many L&D teams don't have the luxury of bringing in expert talent. This doesn't mean you have to become a data scientist to get started. Instead, find the really smart data people that work within your company and buy them lunch. Building relationships with your business operations and human resource partners is a great place to start your journey toward improved data practices. Pick their brains to improve your understanding of how the organization uses data and how L&D may be able to take advantage of existing resources. Then, do your homework and improve your foundational data knowledge. This will help you ask better questions and make informed decisions as you apply the MLE Framework to finally fix learning measurement.

By the way, you probably already figured out that there is no such thing as the Van Pelt Learning Measurement Model. Lucy Van Pelt is a friend of Charlie Brown who always pulls the football away at the last moment and offers cheap-and-unqualified psychiatric advice for neighborhood kids. Last time I checked, she did not grow up to become an L&D professional.

Roger Kaufman, Valerie Anderson, Robert Brinkerhoff, Jack Phillips, and Will Thalheimer, on the other hand, all developed evaluation methods, many of which take inspiration from The Kirkpatrick Model:

- Kaufman's Five Levels of Evaluation
- Anderson's Value of Learning Model

- Brinkerhoff's Success Case Method
- Phillips's ROI Methodology
- Thalheimer's Learning Transfer Evaluation Model

Check out each of these frameworks and borrow elements to create your own right-fit measurement strategy.

Chapter 13

Mastering the Game of Influence

Get Stakeholder Buy-In for Your Awesome New Idea

SPOILER ALERT

We're going to talk about practical steps you can take to change people's mindsets when it comes to the value of workplace learning. Let's dive into the Game of Influence, including:

- How and why to play the game
- The players you should invite to the game
- Proven tactics you can use to win

Which of the following statements do you think is more likely to gain interest from an executive stakeholder?

I have a new idea that will revolutionize our workplace learning strategy!

or

I can make sure our people have the skills needed to execute our business priorities without disrupting the operation.

Both statements could easily be used to explain the same concept. However, the second statement is infinitely more appealing. In fact, I've used this exact statement countless times to successfully sell the business case for modern learning tactics like microlearning within Fortune 1000 companies.

As L&D pros, we must accept a fundamental truth: Learning is our thing. We're the people within our organizations who spend time discussing topics like pedagogy, e-learning, and performance support. We're the ones who go to conferences and read books (thanks again) on this stuff. Workplace learning strategy may be super exciting for us, but it's usually a means to an end to the people we support. We must keep this reality top of mind if we hope to architect disruption-ready learning ecosystems.

At the same time, we must acknowledge that we can't get anything done without our partners. L&D doesn't control the audience, and we can't make unilateral decisions about how people do their jobs. We're one of many support teams vying for people's time and attention at work. Whether we're launching a new program, implementing technology, or gathering participant feedback, we need buy in and support from stakeholders across the organization. Unfortunately, when people have an antiquated mindset regarding the value of workplace learning, getting that buy in can be a lot more difficult than it should be.

What's Your Job Again?

Do you have a hard time explaining what you do for a living to people outside L&D?

I sure do! It's always fun to hear other people explain my job. Sometimes I'm a teacher. Sometimes I'm a marketing professional. Sometimes I'm a video producer. And sometimes I'm an IT person (and subsequently get plenty of "can you fix my . . ." questions). Over the years, I've found myself playing all those roles in service of helping people do their jobs better. This is a testament to the wide range of skills required within a modern L&D team—sometimes within individual roles. Large talent development functions may have the resources to hire dedicated content developers, instructional designers, project managers, data scientists, systems administrators, and facilitators. However, if you're a mighty L&D department of 40 supporting 400,000 people, you're probably wearing several hats at any given time.

This lack of role clarity often carries over within our organizations. Stakeholders know us (and therefore judge our value) based on their most recent interactions with our solutions. To some, we're the compliance people who force them to do that boring e-learning program once per year. To others, we're the team that runs the off-site programs with the really good lunches. Yes, these examples are some of the more extreme misjudgments we often encounter, but you must admit there are plenty of stakeholders at every level of the organization who think this is what L&D is supposed to do. Why should we expect them to invite us into their strategic conversations or be open to innovative new ideas when they have such expansive mindset gaps when it comes to workplace learning?

Shifting Mindsets

This book is worthless if you're not able to shift the way people think about learning at work. Educating employees on a new product is easy when compared to changing the way they think about learning after years of schooling and job training. To effectively apply the MLE Framework, you must break the long-held belief that all learning activities must follow the same structure: course → test → complete. Otherwise, stakeholders will keep coming back with ill-informed requests and your organizational impact will be limited. L&D must find a way to help people realize that a 90-minute instructor-led training session is almost never the right-fit solution for a complex performance problem.

I know it's frustrating. You're the expert. No one is pushing the accountants to do their jobs in a way that clashes with fundamental principles. But the accountants also don't ask for people's attention on a regular basis. Learning requires effort. Traditional training tactics, like classroom sessions and online courses, disrupt the operation, especially in workplaces with limited staffing. The MLE Framework addresses this problem by making learning an embedded part of the workflow, but stakeholders don't know that. They only know what they've experienced in the past when it comes to job training. As a result, they often view L&D as a distraction that doesn't provide a clear ROI. When I was an operations manager, I was always annoyed when the training team "borrowed" my team members during busy days. When they got back, they were never noticeably better at their jobs. What could the value of this training possibly have been for my operation, and why should I go along with it when I have KPIs for which I'm held responsible as a manager?

Trust is the foundation of a modern learning mindset. People must trust that L&D has their best interests in mind as we recommend and implement solutions, especially if these solutions don't match past experiences. But building trust is not a one-size-fits-all proposition. L&D must navigate an ever-changing maze of stakeholders, decision makers, and subject matter experts, all of whom come to the table with their own interests, goals, and motivations. Shifting long-held beliefs is a complicated process that requires long-term vision. As Denzel Washington's character in *Training Day* so eloquently put it "This sh*t's chess, it ain't checkers." To build a modern learning organization, L&D pros must master the Game of Influence.

The Players

Workplace learning touches every employee within an organization, so L&D must be ready to play with every possible influencer. Your stakeholders will vary based on the scope of your mandate and the audiences you support. Let's profile some of the most common L&D stakeholders.

The Executive

 This player drives results. They're accountable to shareholders, board members, regulators, and public perception (as well as employees). Some execs, especially those on the operational side of the business, may recognize the importance of maintaining a skilled workforce, but many do not understand the ongoing investment required to make this a reality. This is why L&D budgets are usually one of the first to get cut when execs push for cost savings.

To gain buy-in from the executive, you must demonstrate how continued investment will help the business achieve desired results and shift the perception of L&D from a cost center to a revenue-enabling function.

The Lawyer

 How many lawyers does it take to shut down an L&D initiative? One. No, that wasn't a setup for a pithy lawyer joke. It's a reality for L&D pros who work in highly regulated industries.

Lawyers protect the company. Their job is to mitigate risk while keeping regulators happy. It's a complicated role that makes them skeptical of new ideas that may upset the apple cart (do people still say that?). Many of them know check-the-box training isn't the best way to help people learn, but it's the approach with which they're most familiar and comfortable.

To gain buy-in from the lawyer, you must demonstrate your ability to maintain compliance within your reimagined strategy. This includes checking all the boxes this player needs to get their job done.

The IT Pro

 This player also protects the company. They establish hardware and software guidelines to keep data secure, reduce costs, and eliminate redundancies. They want to keep the list of approved technologies short while making sure employees have the tools needed to do their jobs. They operate with minimal resources, most of which are focused on customer-facing projects. This means they always have limited bandwidth for internal requests, including L&D initiatives.

To gain buy-in from the IT pro, you must demonstrate how you will follow the rules while providing meaningful, differentiated solutions that deliver business value.

The SME

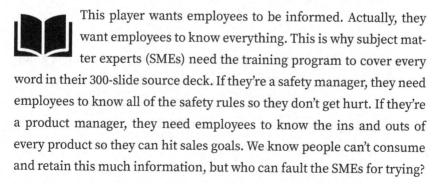 This player wants employees to be informed. Actually, they want employees to know everything. This is why subject matter experts (SMEs) need the training program to cover every word in their 300-slide source deck. If they're a safety manager, they need employees to know all of the safety rules so they don't get hurt. If they're a product manager, they need employees to know the ins and outs of every product so they can hit sales goals. We know people can't consume and retain this much information, but who can fault the SMEs for trying?

To gain buy-in from the SME, you must demonstrate your ability to cover all of the required information within your learning strategy.

The Manager

 This player "doesn't have time for learning." They have limited staffing, limited resources, and KPIs they gotta hit. If they don't immediately see how training will help them achieve their goals, they won't support it. If they don't make training a team priority, it won't get done—no matter how much buy-in you have from other stakeholders.

To gain buy-in from the manager, you must demonstrate how your solution will help them achieve their objectives without disrupting the operation.

The Employee

 This player is busy doing their job. Some have autonomy to opt into learning activities. Others are scheduled down to the minute. This player wants to build their skills so they can do their job better, but they're already overloaded with work. If anyone wants to add a new task to their list, they better explain why it's worth the effort. Otherwise, they're not going to do it—at least not until their manager chases them down because their name is on a list. "Because L&D said so" is not a move that works on this player.

To gain buy-in from the employee, you must demonstrate how learning activities relate to their individual needs and make them easy to access within the flow of work.

The Tactics

Every player in this game is unique. Some tactics may work for one group but fall flat with another. Rarely does a single tactic influence everyone on the board. This makes the game a lot more difficult to play—and even more rewarding to win. Here's a list of potential moves (influence tactics) you can make to kickstart a modern learning mindset shift.

Case Study

A good case study explains how another organization achieved results by applying an idea similar to the one you're pitching to stakeholders. A great case study may come from a well-known organization that has a lot in common with your workplace. However, it doesn't always have to come from a company in the same industry or with a recognizable logo. Some stakeholders may be influenced by a case study from an organization they respect, regardless of how dissimilar it may be from their own.

For bonus points, connect your stakeholders with people from the company that participated in the case study so they can provide real-world insight into the effectiveness of your shared idea.

External SMEs

A good idea can sometimes become a great idea when it comes out of someone else's mouth. Sounds ridiculous, right? Let's call this move "the Influencer Gambit." The unfortunate truth is that people get labeled within their own organizations based on their past work. If you propose an idea that's outside your established wheelhouse, stakeholders may immediately dismiss it. However, if you bring in someone from outside the company—someone with an established resume—to pitch the exact same idea, the concept suddenly becomes more credible.

For bonus points, build a network of external SMEs with established authority on concepts related to your L&D transformation efforts just in case you need them along the way.

Reporting

If a stakeholder needs certain boxes checked as part of a training program, show them how you will provide reporting to verify that said boxes have been checked. For example, if you want to transition compliance training from a 60-minute course to a series of microlearning videos, your first move with this stakeholder must be to provide reporting that meets both internal compliance and external regulatory requirements. This will put the stakeholder at ease and make them more amenable to new methods.

For bonus points, entice your stakeholder with the promise of collecting additional data as a result of your new strategy. In the previous microlearning example, you can highlight the option to use reinforcement training to track employee knowledge changes over time as opposed to the traditional one-and-done approach to assessment.

Road Map

All technology requests must include a road map covering key stakeholder requirements, processes, and expectations. For example, your road map for a new learning platform should include:

- Problems that created the need for your request
- How your suggested solution will solve the problems
- Why existing resources are insufficient to solve this problem
- The effort and cost required to implement and maintain your solution
- A process for implementing and maintaining your solution
- How your solution will (or will not) affect existing tools and processes
- How data, security, and governance requirements will be met

A road map will make your solution sound simpler, more strategic, and worthwhile. It shows you've done your homework and care about your stakeholder's concerns. By preempting another player's objections, you make it easier for them to accept your new idea.

For bonus points, apply the road map tactic to ideas that do not focus on technology.

Improv

The two most powerful words in the Game of Influence are "yes, and." This standard practice in improv comedy is also a powerful influencing move. By starting your response to a stakeholder request with "yes," you demonstrate your acceptance of new information as opposed to immediately challenging or dismissing it (even if it's a bad idea). The "and" then allows you to build upon the foundational idea by taking it in a new, complementary direction.

"Yes, and" is a potent long-game influencing tactic (remember, this is chess, not checkers). When a stakeholder comes to you with a pre-baked solution that you know is a bad fit, don't immediately push back. Instead, agree to work with them on the suggested solution, and offer ways to augment it with complementary tactics (the idea you prefer). After implementation, demonstrate the effectiveness of your additional tactics and suggest they be applied during future projects.

For bonus points, give the stakeholder the opportunity to discover the value of your complementary solution on their own, thereby making the innovation their idea instead of yours (you're Alfred, not Batman, right?).

Help

Why should a stakeholder champion a new L&D idea if L&D hasn't helped them do their own job better? In other words, what have you done for me lately? No, I'm not talking about providing stakeholders with special versions of employee training or scheduling them to complete programs first. Instead, you must prioritize your stakeholders as part of your ongoing L&D practices and make sure they receive right-fit support too, before you ask for their help. Shift their mindset by demonstrating your ability to solve their problems. Then, ask them to champion your new initiative.

For bonus points, prove the value of a new concept, such as shared knowledge or performance support, by applying it with a stakeholder group first, before rolling it out to the target audience.

Peer

Who do you trust more: people with flashy titles who you rarely see or the people you work with shoulder-to-shoulder every day? Exactly! Formal authority may force employees to complete training, but it can't make people value learning as part of their jobs. Whenever possible, leverage peer influencers as L&D champions. Run small experiments within peer groups to demonstrate the effectiveness of new tactics. Collect their anecdotal feedback and use it within communications with the larger audience. Show them how people with similar goals, backgrounds, interests, circumstances, and experiences benefitted before asking them to try it themselves.

For bonus points, involve members of your target audiences in every step of the process so they can more effectively communicate the underlying value of your solutions.

Playing the Game

The Game of Influence never ends despite the number of times frustrated players try to flip the board. The good news is that you're already playing the game, whether you realized it or not. The bad news is that you're probably falling behind if you didn't realize the game had already started.

I realized I had to step up my own game when I first introduced the MLE Framework within my contact center operation. I wanted to move away from e-learning as the default L&D solution and adopt an approach grounded in shared knowledge. However, my stakeholders all wanted the same old e-learning content, and I didn't have the political capital needed to say no. So, I went looking for stakeholders who might be open to a shared knowledge approach to problem solving. I found Mike.

Mike was a sales VP. He wasn't the most powerful executive in the company, but he had a solid amount of influence. More importantly, everyone liked Mike. He was well known for the motivational emails he sent to his team at the end of every week that were eventually forwarded all over the company. Even better, people had a habit of replying to Mike to express their appreciation for and agreement with his messages. In other words, this was how they sucked up to their boss.

I approached Mike with an idea. What if he had his own blog within our new knowledge base? He could share his motivational messages from a centralized spot, and people could subscribe, like, and comment without clogging up their inboxes. Of course, Mike jumped on the opportunity. Every Friday, he posted his words of encouragement and recognition on his blog. Like clockwork, people from all over the company popped in to prove that they'd read it. Sure, most of their comments were vapid statements like "Great job, Mike!" and "Couldn't have said it better, Mike!" I didn't care, because they were paying attention to my knowledge base instead of their email. Mike's blog was a big step toward building the credibility needed to make shared knowledge a viable alternative to e-learning. Mike got what he wanted. I got what I needed to kickstart a learning mindset shift. Win/win!

Making the Right Moves

The key to winning the Game of Influence is making your moves as early as possible. Remember, the goal is to build trust and credibility, not just manipulate people to do what you want them to do. Therefore, you must start applying influencing tactics with key stakeholders ASAP to strengthen your relationships well in advance of asking for their help.

Step 1. Clarify Your Objective

It's always a good idea to be a helpful and trusted member of the organization. It's always important to build solid relationships and make sure people enjoy working with you. However, you probably won't have the time to build this kind of relationship with everyone in your company, especially if you work in a large, distributed organization. Therefore, you must determine how strategic influence can help you achieve your goals and determine specific influencing objectives.

In my contact center example, my objective was to increase employee awareness and executive buy-in for our new shared knowledge base as a first step to making it a credible learning solution.

Step 2. Identify Your Stakeholders

Once you know what you want to achieve through stakeholder influence, you must identify the players. With whom should you build or strengthen your relationship to achieve your desired outcome? You may focus on one stakeholder, or you could build a lengthy list of people that may somehow affect your objective. Remember that influence does not always require formal authority. Frontline employees are considerable L&D influencers even if their approval is not required to implement a new strategy.

In my contact center example, I identified Mike and his employee network as stakeholders at this stage of my shared knowledge initiative. I had already applied influencing tactics to gain support from other executives, legal, IT, and L&D months prior.

Step 3. Match Stakeholders to Influence Tactics

Next, you must do your homework to understand your stakeholders. Set up meet and greets. Buy them coffee and ask about their work. Speak with partners who have experience working with the same stakeholders. You'll quickly discover that the same tactic is unlikely to work for everyone. Each stakeholder has their own motivations, responsibilities, interests, and goals. Therefore, you must select right-fit tactics that ensure both you and the stakeholder get equal value from your relationship.

This is why the sample statement from the beginning of this chapter is such a powerful influence tactic:

> I can make sure our people have the skills needed to execute
> our business priorities without disrupting the operation.

This one sentence aligns L&D value (building skills) with executive stakeholder value (executing business priorities) while proactively addressing potential concerns (operational disruption).

Table 13-1 shows how I selected the right tactics based on my selected stakeholders within my contact center example.

Table 13-1. Aligning Tactics to Stakeholders

Stakeholder	Motivation	Tactic	Value
Executive (Mike)	Build connection with distributed team through messages of motivation and appreciation	Provide a more engaging way to deliver team messages	Get an influential executive hands-on within the new knowledge base
Employees	Gain approval from a senior executive while maintaining operational awareness	Provide a simpler, more visible way to engage with executive messages	Build an employee habit of using the new knowledge base as part of the workflow

Step 4. Implement and Evaluate

Influence is not a one-and-done concept. You must continue to nurture your stakeholder relationships after you apply your initial tactics. For example, you may set a cadence for regular check-ins by using calendar reminders (it's not just for remembering birthdays). You must also continue to assess the stakeholder landscape and make adjustments as needed. If a stakeholder leaves the company or a new regulation is released, you must proactively determine how this may affect your ability to get work done and introduce new tactics if necessary.

I continued to collaborate with Mike to evolve his blogging strategy. I measured engagement on his posts and provided him with a monthly report. The success of this tactic led us to expand our use of champion contributors within our knowledge base. Eventually, more than 250 stakeholders were building content for their audiences while increasing the credibility and depth of our solution.

Winning the Game

Building trust isn't a game, despite the metaphor used in this chapter. We're talking about developing human relationships, not just manipulating players on a board. It's a long, challenging, and essential process. It can be simultaneously rewarding and frustrating, especially when company politics come into play. That's why I went with the game motif. It makes the concept more fun to discuss and adds a critical strategy layer to the conversation.

Plus, there's one more particularly cool part about the Game of Influence: Everyone must win. Stakeholders must derive clear value from L&D initiatives while L&D gets the support needed to shift people's mindsets and make a real impact.

The MLE Framework represents a significant departure for many learning organizations. It requires you to push back against prebaked, wrong-fit solutions in favor of a systems approach to learning and support. It includes the introduction of new learning tactics, such as reinforcement, as well as the reimagination of familiar methods. This is why

I've never walked into an executive meeting and proclaimed, "I have an idea that will revolutionize our learning strategy!" I realized that changing long-held beliefs about the role of learning in the workplace was going to require a lot more than a PowerPoint presentation. But I also knew (and I hope you agree) that shifting this collective mindset is essential for meeting the demands of the ever-changing workplace. And that makes this long game worth playing.

Chapter 14

Making the Shift

Start Building a Learning Culture That's Ready for Anything

SPOILER ALERT

We're wrapping things up with some suggestions on how to start applying what you've learned in this book, including:
- How to find the balance between disruption and opportunity in workplace learning
- How to begin reshaping your L&D strategy using the MLE Framework

Was I correct when I said this book wasn't about learning?

Learning has been an important part of our story, but it's not the reason we do what we do every day. It's not the problem organizations need our help to solve. Remember: No one goes to work to learn. In fact, learning is usually seen as an obstacle, especially when the provided solutions don't fit within the everyday reality of the workplace.

People go to work for one reason: to do the job. Today, "doing the job" may mean selling enough wireless packages to meet quota, picking and shipping tires to fulfill every customer order, or designing a go-to-market plan for a new software product. Tomorrow, what it takes to successfully "do the job" may change. L&D must provide the support needed to help people keep up with change and perform at their best. Sometimes people need to develop a complex new skill. Often, they just need a quick answer to a question. L&D must architect a flexible support infrastructure capable of balancing both sides of the workplace equation.

Restoring Balance

Disruption and *opportunity* are the two most important words in L&D.

Disruption is an everyday reality. There's always going to be a new product, process, regulatory requirement, or safety consideration. In some cases, disruption creates new opportunities. When my past employer "right sized" half the company out the door, I was faced with the challenge of supporting more departments with fewer L&D resources. This provided me with the unexpected opportunity to learn new parts of the business and experiment with unfamiliar L&D tactics, including shared knowledge and reinforcement. Without that disruptive moment in my career, I may have never adopted a modern learning mindset, implemented the MLE Framework, or written this book.

At the same time, disruption can hold people back from exploring new opportunities. People need time, energy, and resources to take the next step forward, whether that means pursuing their next roles or making big career changes. For example, my friend's company offered low-to-no-cost degrees as a benefit for their frontline staff. However, her job as a restaurant server required her to work long, physically draining hours late at night. She also had to pick up extra shifts most weeks to keep up with her living expenses and student loans. These disruptive demands kept her from finishing her degree for almost a decade, despite the opportunity afforded by her employer and her desire to advance her education. How often do you plan to set aside time for professional development only to get sidetracked by the latest fire drill?

This dichotomy between disruption and opportunity applies to entire organizations too. When companies spend most of their time, effort, and resources trying to fend off competitors or just getting the basics right, they're unable to look ahead, identify promising new trends, and seize future-focused opportunities. Companies like Blockbuster, Blackberry, Kodak, and MySpace failed because they were unable or unwilling to balance the forces of disruption and opportunity. Their short-term thinking caused them to become anchored to their traditional business practices (late fees, keyboards, film, Tom). As a result, they were unable to adapt to the changing marketplace. This allowed competitors like Netflix, Apple, Sony, and Facebook/Meta to quickly overtake them despite their established market dominance.

When you think about it, traditional L&D is a lot like Blockbuster Video in the early 2000s. For a long time, we were the only game in town, just like Blockbuster. If stakeholders wanted to put together a training program, they always came to us—just like people had to go to Blockbuster if they wanted to watch a movie on-demand. And just like Blockbuster, L&D has fallen behind when it comes to leveraging new technology to adapt its operating model. Suddenly, people have options. Departments can implement their own solutions without involving L&D at all. Blockbuster tried to catch up and started shipping DVDs to customers' homes, just like Netflix. They launched their own streaming service, just like Netflix. But by then, simply catching up to the market wasn't enough. Customers had already moved on, and Blockbuster was no more.

Companies may not be close to shuttering their L&D departments like old Blockbuster stores, but they're demanding a new approach that fits the needs of today's workplace. Executives recognize the importance of building the skills needed to execute future-focused business strategies, but they also realize most employees aren't ready to take on new roles (Deloitte 2021). At the same time, pandemic-induced disruption has made it harder than ever to recruit and retain workers. This is forcing managers to once again prioritize operations over training. As a result, 46 percent of employees have seen a reduction in their skill development opportunities (Degreed 2021).

If L&D truly wants to become a strategic function, we must solve this chicken-or-egg problem. We must provide timely support to address today's biggest problems while also enabling the ongoing skills development needed to power future success. L&D must restore the balance between disruption and opportunity so the people and organizations we support can be successful today and tomorrow.

Your Next Steps

So now all you have to do is shift the mindset of your entire organization, reimagine your learning practices, and close the yawning opportunity gap within your workplace so the people you support are ready for whatever comes next. Simple, right? Of course it's not!

Frankly, it would be a lot easier to stick to our comfort zones and keep pumping out instructor-led sessions, webinars, and e-learning modules upon request. The problem with the laissez faire approach is that L&D will not make the decision to transform L&D. Stakeholders—the people who shape our mandate—are making this decision for us, especially if they're forced to seek out their own solutions because we're unable to meet their needs. L&D must resolve the crisis of purpose we discussed earlier in this book. We may still find it hard to explain what we do at high school reunions, but we must find a way to clearly articulate the value of the L&D function. Suffice to say, it's going to take a lot more time and effort than simply changing our titles again.

The MLE Framework provides L&D with a great starting point. It will help you rework how you apply your existing tactics while also expanding your L&D toolkit. You can still facilitate instructor-led sessions. You can still deliver webinars. You can still design e-learning. The MLE Framework will help you apply these tactics in ways that align with how people actually learn, develop, and solve problems on the job.

The disruption brought by the pandemic forced every organization to rethink their employee experiences. It forced companies to make changes that were previously considered impossible, such as shifting to 100 percent remote workforces. Now we know what we're capable of when it comes to reimagining the fundamentals of how work gets done. As organizations reshape the future of work, L&D must be right there reshaping the future of learning and development.

But first, you must assess your L&D maturity and take the appropriate next steps.

1. Share the MLE Framework With Your L&D Peers

Pass this book around within your team (or strongly recommend everyone buy their very own copy—thanks!). Identify the concepts that most relate to the challenges you face within your L&D function and start conversations during team meetings. Present ideas like the MLE Framework and Modern Learning Mindset during internal summits. Heck, you could even invite me to host a session with your team! After all, it often helps to bring an outside perspective to validate your own ideas (the influencer gambit).

2. Find Champions Who Already Think Differently

The L&D function is just the first stop on your mindset transformation tour. Rather than jumping straight to an executive presentation, find people within your workplace network who are commonly open to new ideas. They may be subject matter experts with whom you often work or managers who are always open to piloting new concepts. Share the MLE Framework with them to get their feedback and understand how this approach can help solve their performance challenges.

3. Nail Your Audience Personas

Make sure you know the people you support. Build out detailed personas for each group, including factors like motivation, access, function, location, and time. Compare what you learn about your audience to your existing learning strategies to find any obvious gaps or mismatches. For example, are you relying on 30-minute e-learning modules with an audience that only has 10 minutes available for training in their average workday? Share these personas with your L&D peers to make sure everyone is on the same page.

4. Assess Your Existing Learning Ecosystem

Inventory your learning and support tactics. This may include technologies, content formats, or delivery methods. Align each tactic with the corresponding layer within the MLE Framework. Determine which layers are most represented, along with those that are limited or completely missing. Identify potential methods for closing these gaps. For example, if you're light on shared knowledge tactics, look outside L&D for ways to help people access information on demand, such as the company intranet or team wikis.

5. Play "What If" With Your Current Solutions

Before you start applying the MLE Framework on new projects, practice by reimagining a few past solutions. Collaborate with peers to work through recent projects using the processes discussed in this book. Would you have been able to provide a more right-fit solution using these principles? Are there certain elements of an MLE solution, such as reinforcement or performance support, that would not have been possible with your existing resources? Share your new solution outlines with project champions to get their feedback on how they would have responded to these alternative concepts.

6. Adopt a Results-First Approach to Solution Design

You may have several gaps to close within your ecosystem before you can apply the full framework. However, you can get a head start by switching to a results-first design process while still using your existing tactics. List key questions L&D must ask during each step of the process, such as how the business impact of a solution will be measured. Familiarize stakeholders and SMEs with this approach to identifying right-fit solutions, especially if they typically default to tactics like classroom training.

7. Start Using "Yes, and" to Shift Mindsets

Just because your L&D team buys into the MLE Framework doesn't mean every stakeholder is going to jump onboard. You may be required to deliver solutions you think aren't the best fit for your audience or the challenge they're facing. In these instances, suggest additional tactics that demonstrate the potential for future MLE solutions. For example, legal may require a classroom session for a compliance topic. Suggest augmentative shared knowledge, performance support, or reinforcement tactics using a "yes, and" influencing method. Measure the reaction and impact related to your additional tactics to help build credibility for switching to an MLE approach.

8. Share Early Success Stories

Capture results from any projects that include MLE solutions. Share these stories with other stakeholders and subject matter experts before they come to you with new training requests. Use evidence rather than theory to open their minds to a new approach. Be sure to collect anecdotal feedback from employees, managers, and other stakeholders who participate in these solutions. If people are unwilling to accept new ideas directly from L&D, they may change their tune when presented with feedback from those who work in similar roles and experience similar challenges.

The MLE Framework is designed to help you provide more impactful, right-fit solutions for the people you support. It helps you reframe the problems that arise within your organization and ask better questions during the solutioning process. This repositions L&D from an order-taking cost center to a performance-focused strategic partner.

The Future of Workplace Learning

My last name is Dillon, not Connor. I don't own a Cloak of Levitation. I still can't buy plutonium in every corner drugstore. In other words, I can't predict the future.

Thankfully, I'm not alone. No one really knows what's coming next, regardless of how many "future of" articles pop up online. This is why so many predictions about the "future of learning" are connected to consumer technology trends. It was obvious that the internet would impact the workplace, so it was once declared the future of learning. Then smartphones changed how we live our lives, so clearly they'd also impact the way we learn, right? Then it was Facebook. Then Second Life. Then Netflix. Then TikTok. Today, it's the metaverse.

Learning technology has certainly evolved over the past 25 years. However, the continued reliance on instructor-led training shows just how little it has transformed core L&D practices. Tech has allowed organizations to shift from telling people what to do in a room to telling them what to do on Zoom. We must get better at leveraging tech to move our practices forward, but we can't rely on it to point the way.

The nightmare that was 2020 reinforced the fact that the future of workplace learning is the future of work. L&D must be willing and prepared to adapt its practices to changes in how people work. This includes everything from physical location to the skills required to do the job successfully. Unfortunately, performance challenges aren't going to stop so we can rework our learning strategies. L&D must establish a flexible infrastructure that allows us to build and rebuild the talent development plane as we continue to fly it. The fundamentals of how people learn (the science stuff) will stay the same, but L&D pros must adapt how they engage with their audiences to better align with the realities of how work is done.

This is the future of workplace learning. It's not digital. It's not remote. It's not hybrid. It's ubiquitous. It's personal. It's equitable. It's the opportunity to get the help that you need—anytime, anywhere—to overcome whatever disruption with which you're currently dealing. It's making sure that everyone we work with, from the frontline to the C-suite, recognizes that:

> An organization can only transform as fast as it's people
> can learn.

And it's having the wisdom, insight, and courage to shift our mindsets, step out of our comfort zones, and challenge expectations so the people we support are provided with the tools and resources needed to get ready for whatever comes next.

Are you ready to make the shift?

Epilogue
Find Out What Happened
After the Story Ended

You finished the book!

Thanks again for taking the time to read it, even if you borrowed it from a co-worker instead of buying your own copy. Who needs residuals, right?

So now what? Of course, I really hope you're able to apply as many concepts as possible within your organization to reshape your learning ecosystem and improve employee performance in measurable ways. But what about the book itself? What's gonna happen to it?

Well, if you have the printed version, you'll probably stick it on a shelf with the other great learning and performance books you've read over the years. If you're reading the digital version, it'll likely blend in among the throng of titles on your Kindle bookshelf.

That's the problem with a book. It's a monument—a permanent record of how an author viewed their work at a specific moment in time. This book reflects my perspective on workplace learning in 2022. But who knows how I'll think about my work by the time you read it?

I'm 99 percent sure the MLE Framework will still be the foundation of everything I do in L&D. It's proven effective time and time again for the past decade through a variety of roles and challenges. That said, I have tweaked and iterated the framework along the way based on everything I've learned. It took a lot of trial and error to land on those six particular blocks. What happens if I come up with a new idea that inspires me to change the framework? I could release a new version of this book, but that doesn't help you when your copy is sitting on a shelf in the background of your MS Teams meetings.

That's why you should hit this QR code with your smartphone. It'll take you to LearnGeek.co/mle, the online hub for everything to do with the Modern Learning Ecosystem Framework.

Think of this as your end credit scene, but for a book instead of a movie. You just spent three exhilarating hours on an adventure with the Avengers. Now the story you came for is all wrapped up, and you're super curious about what's going to happen next. That's what you'll find when you hit the link above.

I have lots of ideas for follow-up materials. Who knows what will be there by the time you find the link? Plus, if I make any major changes to the framework, I'll share the latest details on the hub.

I know what you're thinking. Yes, you can share the link with your peers, even if they didn't buy their own copies of the book. But remember—you can't just jump into the Marvel Cinematic Universe at *Avengers: Endgame* and expect to know what's going on. You totally need to watch the 21 movies that came before it to really prove you're a fan. Bonus: It probably didn't take you almost 46 hours to read this book!

Thanks again for reading my book, and I hope you enjoy the supplemental online content. Let's connect to keep the conversation going. I feel like I've been talking at you for hours at this point. Hit me up on LinkedIn, Twitter, or email anytime. I'm always happy to chat.

Be well.

JD

LinkedIn: linkedin.com/in/jddillon

Twitter: twitter.com/JD_Dillon

Email: jd@learngeek.co

References

Accenture. 2019. *Breaking Through Disruption*. Accenture Research.
accenture.com/_acnmedia/thought-leadership-assets/pdf
/accenture-breaking-through-disruption-embrace-the-power-of
-the-wise-pivot.pdf.

Accenture. 2021. *Business Futures 2021 Report*. Accenture Research.
accenture.com/us-en/insights/consulting/_acnmedia/Thought
-Leadership-Assets/PDF-4/Accenture-Signals-Of-Change-Business
-Futures-2021-Report.pdf.

Arets, J., C. Jennings, and V. Heijnen. 2016. *70:20:10 Towards 100%
Performance*. Maastricht, the Netherlands: Sutler Media.

ATD (Association for Talent Development). nd. "Talent Development
Glossary Terms." ATD. td.org/glossary-terms.

ATD (Association for Talent Development). 2021. *2021 State of the
Industry*. Alexandria, VA: ATD Press.

Axonify and Arlington Research. 2019. *2019 State of Frontline
Employee Workplace Training*. Axonify. info.axonify.com/2019
-ipsos-report.html.

Axonify and Arlington Research. 2020. *The State of Frontline Employee
Training 2020*. Axonify, September. assets.website-files.com
/5f710828d5352c17f46d2d9a/602dbd505d0384a0ae17007b_The%20
State%20of%20Frontline%20Training2020_Global%20FINAL.PDF.

Axonify and Arlington Research. 2021. *The State of the Frontline Work
Experience 2021*. Axonify, September. axonify.com/state-of
-frontline-work-experience-2021.

Brown, P.C., H.L. Roediger III, and M.A. McDaniel. 2014. *Make It Stick:
The Science of Successful Learning*. Boston: Belknap Press.

Camarota, S.A., and K. Zeigler. 2019. "67.3 Million in the United States Spoke a Foreign Language at Home in 2018." Center for Immigration Studies, October 29. cis.org/Report/673-Million -United-States-Spoke-Foreign-Language-Home-2018

Clement, J. 2020. "Internet Usage Worldwide: Statistics and Facts." Statista, October 26. statista.com/topics/1145/internet-usage -worldwide.

Corporate Research Forum. 2017. *Research Report: Strategic Workforce Analytics*. Corporate Research Forum, March 11. crforum.co.uk /research-and-resources/research-report-strategic-workforce -analytics.

Degreed. 2021. *The State of Skills 2021: Endangered*. Degreed. stateofskills.degreed.com.

Deloitte. 2021. *The Social Enterprise in a World Disrupted: Leading the Shift From Survive to Thrive (2021 Deloitte Global Human Capital Trends)*. Deloitte. deloitte.com/content/dam/insights/us /articles/6935_2021-HC-Trends/di_human-capital-trends.pdf.

Fosway Group. 2021. *The Reskilling Revolution*. Fosway Group. fosway.com /research/next-generation-hr/the-reskilling-revolution.

Gallup. 2021. *State of the American Manager*. Gallup. gallup.com /services/182138/state-american-manager.aspx.

Gottfredson, C., and B. Mosher. 2012. "Are You Meeting All Five Moments of Learning Need?" *Learning Solutions*, June 18. learningsolutionsmag.com/articles/949/are-you-meeting-all-five -moments-of-learning-need.

Gottfredson, C., and B. Mosher. 2022. "The 5 Moments of Need." The 5 Moments of Need. 5momentsofneed.com.

Grand View Research. 2020. "Education Technology Market Size, Share & Trends Analysis Report, By Sector (Preschool, K-12, Higher Education), By End-user (Business, Consumer), By Type, By Deployment, By Region, And Segment Forecasts, 2022–2030." Grand View Research. grandviewresearch.com/industry-analysis /education-technology-market.

Humu. 2022. *State of the Manager Report.* Humu. humu.com/state-of
-the-manager-report-2022.

Insight222. 2021. "HR in the Digital Age: A New Behavioral Profile of
the HR Professional." My HR Future, June. myhrfuture.com/hr-in
-the-digital-age.

Johnson, D. 2014. "Getting from 70-20-10 to Continuous Learning."
Research Bulletin, December 3. Washington, DC: Bersin by
Deloitte. deloitte.com/content/dam/Deloitte/at/Documents
/human-capital/research-bulletin-2014.pdf.

Johnson, D. 2021. *Coaching Tech: The Human and the Robots.* RedThread
Research. redthreadresearch.com/coaching-tech-landscape
-humans-and-robots-comp-version.

Johnson, D., and P. Mehrotra. 2019. *The Art and Science of Designing
a Learning Technology Ecosystem.* RedThread Research.
redthreadresearch.com/wp-content/uploads/2020/07/LTE-Final
-Report-1.pdf.

Kahneman, D. 2013. *Thinking Fast and Slow.* New York: Farrar, Straus
and Giroux.

Karpicke, J.D., and A. Bauernschmidt. 2011. "Spaced Retrieval:
Absolute Spacing Enhances Learning Regardless of Relative
Spacing." *Journal of Experimental Psychology: Learning, Memory,
and Cognition* 37(5): 1250–1257.

Karpicke, J.D., and J.R. Blunt. 2011. "Retrieval Practice Produces More
Learning Than Elaborative Studying With Concept Mapping."
Science 331(6018): 772–775. science.org/doi/10.1126/science.1199327.

LinkedIn Learning. 2018. *2018 Workplace Learning Report.* LinkedIn.
learning.linkedin.com/resources/workplace-learning-report-2018.

Pappas, C. 2015. "The Top LMS Statistics and Facts For 2015 You Need
To Know." *eLearning Industry,* May 26. elearningindustry.com
/top-lms-statistics-and-facts-for-2015.

Pew Research Center. 2021. "Mobile Fact Sheet." Pew Research Center
Fact Sheets, April 7. pewresearch.org/internet/fact-sheet/mobile.

Quinn, C.N. 2018. *Millennials, Goldfish & Other Training Misconceptions: Debunking Learning Myths and Superstitions*. Alexandria, VA: ATD Press.

Roche, P., J. Schneider, and T. Shah. 2020. "The Next Software Disruption: How Vendors Must Adapt to a New Era." McKinsey & Company blog, June 22. mckinsey.com/industries/technology -media-and-telecommunications/our-insights/the-next-software -disruption-how-vendors-must-adapt-to-a-new-era.

Shank, P. 2017. *Practice and Feedback for Deeper Learning: 26 Evidence-Based and Easy-to-Apply Tactics That Promote Deeper Learning and Application*. Colorado Springs: Learning Peaks.

Silver, L. 2019. "Smartphone Ownership Is Growing Rapidly Around the World, but Not Always Equally." Pew Research Center, February 5. pewresearch.org/global/2019/02/05/smartphone-ownership-is -growing-rapidly-around-the-world-but-not-always-equally.

Statista. 2019. "Number of Apps Installed by Mobile Users in the United States as of 3rd Quarter 2019." Statista, October 19. statista.com/statistics/267309/number-of-apps-on-mobile-phones.

Statista. 2021. "Learning Technologies Current Usage in All Companies in the Training Industry in the United States in 2021." Statista, November. statista.com/statistics/796024/learning -technologies-current-usage-in-all-companies-in-the-training -industry-us.

Taylor, D. 2017. *Learning Technologies in the Workplace: How to Successfully Implement Learning Technologies in Organizations*. London: Kogan Page.

Toffler, A. 1970. *Future Shock*. New York: Random House.

Twain, M. 2010. *Mark Twain's Own Autobiography: The Chapters from the North American Review*. Madison, WI: University of Wisconsin Press.

Wikipedia. 2021. "1% Rule (Internet Culture)." Wikipedia, Retrieved on June 30. en.wikipedia.org/wiki/1%25_rule_(Internet_culture).

World Economic Forum. 2020. *The Future of Jobs Report 2020*. World Economic Forum, October 20. weforum.org/reports/the-future-of -jobs-report-2020.

Index

Page numbers followed by *f* and *t* refer to figures and tables, respectively.

effectiveness of, 105–106
examples of, 145, 148–149, 154, 160, 166
and failure of managers, 95–97
overcoming disruption with, 103–104
at Peloton, 99
and poor management, 94
for problem-solving, 100
completion, required, 112
complexity, in results-first design, 136, 144, 148, 152, 159, 164
compliance, 117–120, 125
confidence, employee, 60–61
confidence-based assessment, 79
connection, technology for, 174
consistency
of learning technology, 174
of performance support, 63
content development, 44–45, 179
context
adding local, 100
learning technology for, 174
for reinforcement, 84–85
in results-first design, 135, 144, 147, 152, 158, 164
continuous learning model, 4–5, 4f
contribution, time to, 60
Corporate Research Forum, 196
COVID-19 pandemic
adapting to change during, 11
coaching during, 103–104
disruption during, xiii, 225, 226
information during, 64
learning technology during, 170–171
shared knowledge during, 45
skills gaps during, 17
criticality, in results-first design, 135–136, 144, 152, 164
culture
coaching, 104
learning (See learning culture)
curation mindset, 125
curators, 44, 48–49

D
data
to coach effectively, 103
continuous measurements of, 195–208
finding the right, 202–204
good, 201–202
leveraging, 197
as microlearning principle, 114, 116
for persona-based learning, 184
problems related to, 196–198
data component, 179–180
data-enabled function, 200–201
data sources, 105
decision making, 13–14
Degreed, 17
delivery tools, for reinforcement, 87
Deloitte, 17, 85
digital component, 182–183
digital gap, 20
digital learning ecosystem, 183–184. *See also* technology, learning
Dirksen, Julie, 72
disruption, xi–xiv
coaching to overcome, 103–104
during COVID-19 pandemic, 225, 226
for L&D, 7–8
and learning technology, 193–194
managers' ability to overcome, 95
and opportunity, 224–225
performance support to overcome, 64–65
reinforcement to overcome, 85–86
shared knowledge to overcome, 45
Duolingo, 80, 82

E
ecosystem(s)
digital learning, 183–184
learning, 13, 227–228
mapping, 129–130
in MLE framework, 27–31
persona-based digital learning, 175–184

education, value of, 192
employees
    at center of learning experience, 31
    development of, 101–102
    as players to influence, 214
engagement, 191, 205, 205*f*
equity, 175
evaluating influence tactics, 221
executives, 212
expectations, coaching, 104–105
experience component, 176, 178–179
experience(s)
    designing shared knowledge, 50
    scale of personal, 14
experimentation
    in MLE framework, 25
    of reinforcement strategies, 87–88
    to solve shared knowledge
        problems, 50

F

failure
    coaching to prevent, 95–97
    learning from, 83
    of traditional learning
        measurement, 199–200
familiarity (microlearning principle),
    114, 115
features, capabilities vs., 181
firehose method of training, 81
5 moments of need, 5–6, 5*f*
focus (microlearning principle), 114
food safety example, 162–167
forgetting curve, 75*f*, 77–79, 79*f*
formal training. *See* pull and push
    training
format (microlearning principle),
    114, 116
Fosway Groups, 17

G

Gallup, 94–96
Game of Influence, 218–222
Google Maps, 59–60

Gottfredson, Conrad, 5, 58
governance, data, 206

H

hand-raising tactics, 66
helping others, 217
honesty, 120
Humu, 98

I

impact
    business, of learning solution,
        14–15
    measuring, 66, 197–198
    technology's value and, 192
inclusion gap, 20
influence, 209–222
    factors for building, 210–218
    game of, 218–222
    tactics for building, 214–218
information. *See also* shared
    knowledge
    access to, 41
    retaining, 62
information sharing platforms, 37
innovation, 192
input, data, 179–180
insight, for coaches, 97, 98, 105
instructor-led training, 229–230
integration, 189–190, 189*f*
interleaving, 78
interoperability, 206
IT professionals, 213

J

Jennings, Charles, 3
job performance, compliance and, 119
job training, 117, 118
Johnson, Dani, 4

K

Kahneman, Daniel, 82
Kaufman, Roger, 207

veracity of data, 201
volume of data, 201

W
Wallace, Guy, 59
Walt Disney World Resort, xi–xii,
    67–70, 107–110, 128
warehouse safety example, 142–145
whiteboardification, 26–27
winning the game, 221–222
Work Economic Forum, 18–19
workflow, 12, 65, 128
World Economic Forum, 17

Y
"yes, and" technique, 216–217, 228–229

About the Author

JD Dillon is a lifelong Philadelphia Flyers fan, which means he's a master of overinflated expectations and soul-crushing disappointment. He can recite all the words from the first *Back to the Future* movie but didn't bother to learn the lines from the sequels because they aren't nearly as good.

Professionally, JD's 20+ year career is split into three phases. First, he worked in operations and HR management with companies like AMC and Disney. He then transitioned into L&D leadership roles, first with Disney before moving on to Kaplan. Now, he's on the technology side of workplace learning and performance as Axonify's Chief Learning Architect where he builds products and services used on the job by millions of employees around the world.

JD is a respected author, keynote speaker, podcaster, and online host with a passion for helping people do their best work every day. He specializes in enabling frontline workers in industries like retail, grocery, finance, logistics, hospitality, manufacturing and plenty more.

JD is also the founder of LearnGeek, through which he publishes a variety of content and advises organizations on their learning, performance and technology strategies. He graduated from the University of

Central Florida with degrees in communications and marketing. He has an MBA from Kaplan University.

You can find JD riding his Peloton, refusing to stand in line for rides at theme parks in Orlando, or online at LearnGeek.co.